# FRAGMENTS OF REALITY

# FRAGMENTS OF REALITY

## Daily Entries of Lived Life

*Peter Cajander*

iUniverse, Inc.
New York Lincoln Shanghai

# FRAGMENTS OF REALITY
Daily Entries of Lived Life

iUniverse books may be ordered through booksellers or by contacting:

iUniverse
2021 Pine Lake Road, Suite 100
Lincoln, NE 68512
www.iuniverse.com
1-800-Authors (1-800-288-4677)

*Cover design by Jussi Tapaninen.*

ISBN-13: 978-0-595-37522-6 (pbk)
ISBN-13: 978-0-595-81915-7 (ebk)
ISBN-10: 0-595-37522-7 (pbk)
ISBN-10: 0-595-81915-X (ebk)

Printed in the United States of America

# Contents

# Preface

This book is an insight into a period in my life that was very intense. Each evening, I wrote about the day's experiences and insights. My daily life was the raw material for the thoughts and extended understanding that followed. Maybe it is worthwhile to remark that from the beginning, this diary format was meant for a larger audience. Therefore, I have not written about the circumstances or situations that led to these writings. They are not relevant in this context, but I can assure you that this period was definitely a rough ride—a lot happened, and not all of it was pleasant or joyous. On the other hand, I seriously doubt that these writings would have the same feeling and depth without the rich raw material of volatile and dynamic daily experiences.

The writings have been sorted under a few titles to make them easier to read. I feel it is important to let the text speak for itself and transmit the ideas as genuinely as possible. Since the material for this book was written within a relatively short period of time, the various topics are partly interlinked and also implicitly referred to, but it is not necessary to follow the suggested order.

This was my exploration for the harmony and tranquility that await everyone. They are with us at all times—we just have to reach for them. There is no better time to start than right now. The busier your life is, the better your chances to experience and explore the opportunities. Internal harmony is not dependent on situations. My insights were gathered from busy daily activities filled with meetings, traveling, conferences, and social functions. Life is always an adventure, and it is not about external circumstances but internal experiences.

Inspiring moments!

Peter Cajander
September 29, 2005
New York

# Belief System

# Ignorance

*Way to see,*
*hear,*
*taste,*
*feel,*
*know,*
*and live the world;*
*With good intentions,*
*limited knowledge,*
*poor perception,*
*lacking observation*
*but still trying.*

*Without shame,*
*or humbleness,*
*knowing,*
*acting,*
*and behaving*
*with certainty,*
*rightness,*
*a sense of pride,*
*and justification,*
*no shadow of doubt,*
*or sign of imperfectness.*

*The wise will know,*
*acknowledge,*
*and let go.*
*Help with patience,*
*love,*
*and kindness.*

*We will learn,*
*and see the world,*
*in a way of perfectness,*
*with no trace of selfishness.*

# Fixed Mind

We like certainty. We would love to live in a world where things are predictable. Or do we?

Our behavior seems to support the idea of predictable life. We do not like to change, and we like surprises even less so. We are comfortable with our ordinary lives and our daily routines and events. We feel that we are in control of our lives. We can manage life.

But all this is an illusion. We are only fooling ourselves. Nothing is the same, ever. We create the static picture in our mind and refuse to observe the world as it is. And the idea of being in control lasts as long as anything outside of our comfort zone does not happen.

Why is it so difficult to adopt and accept that everything flows? We use lots of energy to categorize and squeeze our perception of the world into a frame and into predictable patterns. We create expectations and illusions, which are always broken. And then we get disappointed. Again and again.

How about accepting the uncomfortable fact that we are not in control? Just take life as it comes, without any expectations—humbly. Less sorrow and far fewer surprises. Everything is new, and nothing is surprising. Every day is an adventure and brings something new and exciting. No need to fear anything since uncertainty and change are realized facts of living, like breathing. One can worry less and concentrate more on living. One moment at time with a flexible mind.

# Belief Structures

Our belief structures define who we are and how we interpret the world. They are our point of view and allow us to view the world through rose-colored glasses. We adjust the external world according to our beliefs. Beliefs are our world, and they are us. Hence they are very powerful and have a great impact on us.

When we interact with other people, we interact with their belief structures. If these beliefs are aligned, we feel understood and the interaction is a very pleasant experience. On the other hand, if others' beliefs do not fit into our world, they can threaten or distress us.

We stick to our beliefs. We lock into our bunkers, and try to keep the base safe as long as possible. This is very important because otherwise we are bound to change our understanding of our existence, which often means giving up something and adjusting our life accordingly. We have a huge intolerance for change and uncertainty. Questioning our conventional ways of categorizing and seeing the world imposes an immediate threat for who we believe we are and how the world is constructed according to our understanding.

Until we give up believing and creating thought structures, we are tied up and imprisoned by them. They bound limits to our lives and prevent us from experiencing the external world without filters and mental handicaps.

# Becoming

Often we want something—we want to learn new skills, get rid of bad habits, or change something in our behavior. We are continuously in a state of wanting or becoming. Are we ever getting anywhere?

Wanting (or becoming) states loud and clear that we do not have something. If we had the "something," we would no longer want it. Therefore, wanting is always related to time. It is a declaration that asserts that we are lacking something, and in the future we would desire to change or gain something. But we need time. Or do we?

Unfortunately, we are in a loop. This loop is just the steady state of wanting. The object of wanting changes, but we are always looking at the future. Never is the right time "to be" the something. Instead of wanting, we should act. It is easy to postpone and only want something. And time is our greatest excuse. If we do nothing, it does not just get better with time. If we want something, it requires action right now—never in the future. Every moment we want something means that in that moment we declare that we are not something. How could we be something else if we are saying that we are not? This contradiction results that we are just wanting and getting exactly what we desired—purely want.

The first step is to stop wanting and start to act. For instance, how do you become a gentleman? You simply be one. It is often hard to instantly change your behavior, but the mind-set can be changed immediately. When we stop repeating that we want (i.e., "I'm lacking something") but start to act we are already halfway through. We declare who we are by our actions and then we are.

# Acceptance

We often desire acceptance from others. We are insecure about ourself and need confirmation from other people. We want to know what others might think about us. To be more specific, we are looking for acceptance from others by pondering what others may think about us. In most of the cases, the truth is that others are not thinking about us at all. Why is it so hard to rely on ourself? Why do we continuously worry about how we are perceived by others?

Going after illusions is difficult. Attempting to please others by finding out what they might like or think is just as hard. Our society is full of images and "role models" that describe and broadcast how we should be and what is "in" at the moment. The media carefully follows the young, beautiful, and rich and reports on their every move. People consume these illusions in great numbers. Everybody wants to get his or her share of the "better" life. We want to be associated with and be part of the success—or the illusion—of the greater life. Still, the happiest people are those who find their own way and follow their unique vision. These are the people who set new rules and break the old habits. They create something that has not been done before. They are not afraid to stick out from the crowd.

Following our instinct and finding the inner self is not easy. Since our childhood, we have been raised in the middle of different paradigms, customs, habits, and social expectations. We are expected to behave a certain way and become just like the other people (e.g., successful, famous, etc.). It is hard to realize what it is to be ourself and what we personally want and believe in. René Descartes, one of the most famous Western philosophers, did not accept anything per se. He reconstructed his own perception and understanding of his existence from real metaphysical fact—he might have doubted everything else, but he could not doubt that he existed. From this basis, Descartes started to build his own view of the world, and he only accepted things that he could rationally accept and prove by his own methodology and thinking.

Most of us may not want to be as thorough as Descartes was, but still it is worthwhile to consider and question things around us. Why is a good question to ask for almost everything we do. Often we take things for granted and accept everything at face value. As a result, we have year after year pored over someone else's thoughts and ideas, and we are filled with those; we cannot distinguish ourselves from other people's expectations and points of view. Standing on our own feet and being able to know and live in a way that we really feel is the right way is a wonderful thing. When we get the right choices and answers from within, there is no need to look for acceptance from the outside. It is enough to be satisfied by ourself. Doing the right thing from our own point of view is enough. We can do nothing more than our best in all circumstances. And it is enough, provided that we are honest with ourselves. It does not matter how the others perceive or think about us anymore.

When we start to know ourself, we start to appreciate more of our own actions and life. We are thus happier and can also share the happiness together with other people in our lives. Accepting ourselves and being content with our own lives are the first and the most important steps in our existence. We have to take the first step and do the hard work, but then we can also enjoy the rewards, like Descartes in the seventeenth century.

# Conservatism

We are conservative by nature. We tend to enclose ourselves. Some of the fences we build are physical and more tangible, while others are more abstract. We want to protect ourselves from the outside world and its renewal.

External fences are easier to conceive. They have many faces, from muscle building to creating physical security measures, all the way to building wealth and monetary riches. Mental fences are harder to pinpoint and the most difficult for us to realize. We hide behind our own habits, traditions, mental and conceptual principles and rules, ways of behavior, and subconscious patterns. These mental barriers limit our perception and understanding of the realities of the world. They filter the outside world for us and give us our sense of security and control. But by doing so, they also prevent us from renewing and developing ourselves. Our existence is based on our self-perception, and the fences are guarding us from anything that is not known and familiar to us—the unpleasantness of the external world.

# Busy

We claim to be so busy. What does it really mean, and is it actually possible?

Being busy means that we are occupied at the moment. Therefore, we are intensively carrying out the task at hand and focusing our undivided attention to accomplish this task. If we really are occupied and in a hurry, we need to concentrate and get rid of the tasks one at a time in order to move to the next one. A metaphor from the computer world would be a processor who is either idle or busy, never in between.

In ordinary language, our busyness (any relation to business?) means something else. We mean that we should do or achieve a lot of things in a certain time period. Most of the time, however, we are not actually occupied in a way that requires our undivided concentration and attention. Our busyness has nothing to do with achieving and accomplishing things. We simply mean that there is something in the future we would prefer to be doing than what we are doing at that particular moment. For instance, we have been occupied in a meeting and now we are headed to the next task. We get stuck in traffic, but we are not occupied by the traffic because our mind is urging us to jump ahead and skip this unproductive moment. Being in traffic is something we would rather not do—we would much rather be accomplishing the next task. This is how we are kept "busy." Similarly, when we are finally taking care of the next task, we are often not occupied here either, but thinking about yet another task on our list.

Busyness is our own creation. It has nothing to do with the real world and actual accomplishment and achievement. Busyness simply consumes our time and makes us worry about the future. We trade the current moment for something we have no influence and control over—the unknown future.

We ignore the now time and, above all, get stressed over something we can, at that moment, do nothing about. "Being busy" does not help speed up the traffic while we drive to another meeting or fast forward the current appointment if we would prefer to be at the next occasion. Paradoxically, when we are really accomplishing something that requires our attention, we cannot be busy—we have no time to think about "being busy"—we just carry out the task. Therefore, we should forget the whole concept of busyness and focus on just doing the things we have at hand.

Looking at our daily life from the outset, we are not really occupied. Most of our time goes to moving from one place to another or physically doing something—seldom is our full and undivided attention required to do something. We actually have plenty of time to enjoy the moment and observe the world around us. Stop being busy and occupy yourself for the actual moment—you might even learn something new. Busyness directs our attention to the future, which is just an illusion created by us—it's not real since we can only live in the moment. And you are not busy if you have time to think about being busy.

# Confusion

There is plenty of confusion and chaos around us. Many things seem not to make much sense, and drastic changes happen. Leaving out natural disasters and environmental incidents, humans create much of this confusion.

How does a confused person behave? He or she is insecure and lost in his or her actions. This is literally the case when we are lost in a strange city and wandering around without any clear destination. Confusion in our mind is reflected in our behavior and actions. Similarly, the confusion in the world is a result of the confusion in people's mind. This becomes more apparent by extending the concept of confusion to include ignorance and imperfect perception as well. We have to live in a world with incomplete information and subjective interpretation of the events around us. The more our mind wanders and the less efficient our capabilities of concentration and objective observations are, the less accurate the picture we can construct from the things around us. Naturally, this affects our actions and behavior, which are carried out with the best of intentions. Still, the outcomes can be less honorable when observed by more sophisticated understanding.

The confusion always starts from our thinking. First there is a thought, which then can be reflected in words or directly in actions (or in nonactions). Our life is based on more or less a conscious perception of the world and an interpretation of the events and occurrences on which we react. Most of our everyday thinking happens without us noticing it at all. It's routine-like and "nonexistent" for us. We just act. Still, it is possible to acknowledge our existence every moment and to turn it into active being. By being aware of every moment and action we take (even every thought), we have the possibility to reduce the confusion and become more aware of our behavior and its consequences to our surroundings.

The best way to decrease confusion around us is to start with ourselves and make sure that we, at least, are not increasing the amount of chaos and ignorance in the world. Only after that can we start to consider helping others (if it is relevant anymore after reaching the first goal perfectly).

# Have To versus Can Do

We are often just struggling. Life is something we have to struggle through. We react, and most of the things are just issues that we have to handle. The attitude toward life is that we *have to*. Most of the things we are required to do like we would not have a choice. But what would you do if you could do what you want instead of what you had to?

We can live our entire life with the "I have to" state of mind. But this has a negative connotation and a pessimistic tone. "I'm the victim and all these things fall to me to sort out." This ideology is fine if you like to live this way. Yet it is not necessary to struggle and play the victim all your life. The circumstances may be the same and all the hardship still may be ahead of us, but we can definitely decide which way to deal with them.

It took me awhile to realize this point. I know others who have done this differently and very concretely. I achieved my realization through mental practice; I did it this way because I knew that I could carry it out the hard way if necessary. So it was not just simple lip service or dreaming. I started to go through all the things that I had to do. When I have to do something, it is out of necessity, and this means that I'm forced into the situation—I don't do it willingly. First I went through my list of things I had to do and came to the conclusion that I actually do not have to do anything—at all. I do not even have to die—it will be taken care of automatically when my time is up. So, there is absolutely nothing that I have to do. What now?

Then I started to consider what *I would like to do*. What would be important and meaningful to me? The things you choose do not necessarily need to be fun and easy—but they have to be truly significant to you. You can only give them a meaning and purpose. Step by step, you can start to get an idea of things that you regard as meaningful and things that you can do. Up to this point in your life, if you have lived the right way, by listening to your own intuition, it should not be a surprise that the things you choose during the exercise might be pretty close to the reality you are already living. Naturally, this might not be the case. But there is a fundamental difference now between the old situation and the new one—the approach and the attitude. Before the exercise, you *had to do* things and now you *can do* those things.

Our ordinary life becomes a set of routines that we take for granted. Our lifestyle and the choices we make are like necessities and obvious things that should be. Therefore, our life also starts to feel like a "have-to" achieving competition. When we question the reasons for the things we do and weigh their real purpose and significance, we may see things differently. We start to appreciate the choices we make and things around us. They are not necessities anymore, but things that we enjoy and want to do. And this is a big difference. Previously, we were unhappy carrying out things and feeling bad, but when we have been given the opportunity to do these things and see the purpose and meaning of them, it is a pleasure to contribute and carry them out—even the routine things.

This is a way to process things without any major crises. Naturally, we start to appreciate things when we face choices in a hard way. When we lose our health or have only a few moments to live, we start to see life differently. Suddenly there are not so many things we have to do, but instead things we *can* do. It would be a shame to lose a major part of our life because of the "have to do" attitude, especially when we could do and experience the same things with an open mind and positive joy of accomplishment. The choice is ours.

# Money

Money is just part of the framework. In itself, it is nothing. It is only a convention between people. We have created the concept called money in order to exchange and settle between various activities and services. It is an enabler, not the purpose itself.

Another way of defining money is to say that it is energy. Notes and coins are energy in their physical material sense because they are formed of atoms. But money can be seen as energy concentration in another sense as well. Money presents, directs, facilitates, blocks, and absorbs lots of energy from us. Sometimes we are tight with money and we are struggling to collect every penny and cent to have enough to survive. Collecting and getting money focuses and concentrates our mental and physical energy (effort) in the everyday life, sometimes more, sometimes less. We might desire something that money enables us to achieve. We work hard and long in order to collect enough wealth to do something with it. In other words, we first absorb and accumulate energy and then release it in some other form. While collecting and getting the required amount of money, we are bound to make choices and give up something else. We need to focus our energy to gather money. In this case, money is a manifestation/representation of our accumulated energy.

Wealth can also demand energy from us. People who have great amounts of wealth need to look after it. They have to concentrate their efforts and focus to manage their wealth. It creates obligations and liabilities. Naturally, it is up to us to define these and live accordingly. This is especially demanding when we do not understand the true nature of money and wealth. Money may turn more into a burden than a facilitator.

Money is only what we make of it and how we place ourselves in relation to it. It is neither a good nor a bad thing. It is only a tool. The sole responsibility lies with the user of the money. Do not mix up the means and the objectives. Money is purely an enabler, nothing else. It does not define who we are—only what we have. And everything we can ever have or not have is only part of the framework. The real essence of life is not about having, but about being. What is important is what we are in relation to other living beings—not what we are in relation to material things like money. A wise person is the one who realizes this.

# Opinions

We are quick to have opinions about anything. Even when we lack facts, we get strong feelings about things. We jump to conclusions rather than consider carefully. Our mind works in a manner that "forces" us to take sides. Undecided opinions are not of much value, and you quickly "lose" the conversation if the arguments are not clear and become tilted to one side or the other.

Actually, opinions are totally useless. You can ask one hundred people for their opinions and they will all have different points of view. This is natural because we are all more or less bound to imperfect understanding and perceptions of the world. Therefore, our opinions are based on our own angle and experience. Opinions do not need to be associated with objective facts or knowledge because we simply do not have access to that type of information; we live in a world of imperfect data and perceptions. That is why opinions are so frustrating. We simply do not understand the rationale behind them, and often there is none—we simply feel or "just think so."

There is a big difference between opinions and firsthand experience. The latter is based on our own wisdom—we have knowledge about the issue. It is "true" to us and we have lived through the experience; therefore, we have a stronger standing point and more accuracy to describe the issue. Nevertheless, the absolute truth may not be closer to our reality, but still we are more certain than when talking about opinions. We like to learn from people who speak from their own experience. We feel that they have something of value to offer us. Opinions, on the other hand, are pure lip service. They are recycled words that are not considered and thought true by the speaker. Opinions have no relevance—we could easily live without them. Let's experience more and repeat less what others have done.

# Routines

We love to fixate. We are afraid of new, unknown things. Being novel is maybe the most difficult thing to do. A physical appearance is easy to observe and, therefore, the most visible way to see the patterns and changes, if there are any. Some people never change their hairstyle during their entire lifetime (and they do not have to be bald).

Leaving appearance aside, thinking and acting original is more important. We cling to our routines and thinking—we are lazy about discovering anything new and challenging the status quo. Thinking and questioning requires effort and work. It is easier to fall back on the good old habits and ways of behaving and acting. Unfortunately, this is the way of hurting oneself as well. By refusing to change, we are bound to break our routines once in a while. Some people go nuts, and most of us are just grumping about the extra effort it takes to adjust to the new situation. We are so attached to the old ways of living and the history, and we love routines. We prefer to be boring, predictable, and repetitive machines.

The biggest challenge is to recognize and fight free of all your routines and patterns—to continuously renew. But even renewing can become a habit and routine. The trick is to be fresh and awake every moment, without building any safe havens.

# Rightness

Facts are very important on our time. We live surrounded by lots of information and knowledge. Most of the data around us is not wisdom but more or less processed bits and pieces of information. We are bound to make decisions and jump to conclusions every day. Our understanding and perception is limited, but still we draw conclusions. We pick sides and present our truth as the universal one. Seldom, if ever, do we realize that our subjective point of view is not shared face value by anyone else. It is actually impossible, because everyone has his or her own way of seeing and understanding the world. Our own experiences and knowledge define how we interpret situations and items. Therefore, our own "truth" or rightness is totally unique, subjective.

Still we assume that everybody shares the same values and standards we do. Of course they understand things in a similar manner to the way we understand them. It is so obvious! How can anyone not see the truth and the underlying issues?

This is why it is so easy to say that something is right or wrong. We assume things that do not exist. Actually, it does not matter, because everything is relative. What changes and defines the value weighting are the assumptions out of which the relative judgment is made. These we cannot explicitly define and describe to others—they are embedded in us. If only everybody had the same assumptions and objective facts of the situations and issues, then we could consider making value calls. This is not possible and, therefore, the world is full of chaos and blaming. Everybody is right and wrong at the same time—only in their subjective way. There is no objective absolute truth from which to validate the real standing point.

Rightness is built deep inside us. We need to manifest our excellence and cleverness. We want to demonstrate our capabilities and knowledge. It is important to us to show that we have acknowledged and understood the issue. We want to gain acceptance and recognition from others. Rightness is a very common and often hidden way of achieving this. Seldom is it about the issues themselves— they are just the means for the actual business of getting self-satisfaction. Rightness is often about power struggle and self-justification. We want to prove that we can win and be superior to others, we were right!

A harder lesson to learn is how to acknowledge the rightness of a situation but let it go without having to prove it to others. Another way to express this would be to say that we feel that we have been mistreated or something is unfair. In the situation, we did not have a chance to prove ourselves and show what we regarded as the right thing or proper solution. They may regard us as weak or stupid because we did not claim our position and or stand up for ourselves. Few of us have the guts and the wisdom to give way. The wise do not have to prove anything. Being right itself serves no purpose. It is totally useless and a waste of resources and energy. Why bother with something we already know? Wouldn't it be better to focus on more important issues that bear real significance? Next time you have an inner urge to be right, consider why you are about to act the way you intend to act. Is it purely to achieve the objective or, rather, to prove yourself?

To be right, to be wrong, and just to be. What is the right way?

# Fair and Unfair

Often we feel that we are treated unfairly or something happens that we do not accept as fair. What is fair and what is not?

Life is neither fair nor unfair. It's beyond the concept of "rightness." It does not judge or prefer anything or anyone—it just simply is. How can we still feel that we are mistreated?

When you ask different people about their views of fairness, you get totally different answers. Some find similar circumstances totally acceptable and "right" whereas others see them as totally unacceptable. Someone's fairness is another person's unfairness. This twist can even happen within ourself—over time we may start to see past occurrences differently. So, what has happened then? The situation has not changed because it has already happened (as we recall it). Our own interpretation of it has altered.

We are the only ones who can treat ourselves fairly or unfairly. We put things into a relationship and interpret the outcome. Our understanding is dependent on our own perception, experience, and subjective interpretation of the matter. On top of these, we create our own expectations that project and claim the desired (expected) outcome. Our point of reference is in relation to our expectations. We "judge" the fairness in comparison to how we have perceived and projected the situation. We have certain predetermined plans of the outcome that are formed based on our personal history and knowledge. Therefore, different people can wholeheartedly claim the opposite points of view—everyone lives in his or her own reality.

We evolve over time. Our thinking changes and we perceive the world differently. This is the interplay between our cumulated experiences, understanding, and knowledge that guide us to interpret our surroundings. In other words, our mind continuously seeks to find similarities between personal history and the situation at hand. Naturally, the reality is always fresh and new but depending on our own approach toward it, our personal response and interpretation can vary a great deal. Everything is put into a relationship and we are the only point of reference. What we do not understand, we cannot expect either. Similarly, things that we have a limited experience of can give us great surprises.

We always have to live and respond to the world around us. Still, we do not have perfect information and interpretation available. This creates the churn and drama involved with human life—thanks to our own imperfectness and ignorance. All it takes is us, and it has everything to do with us and nothing to do with third parties or the circumstances surrounding us. The fairness and unfairness are just results of our own thinking and perception and they are in relation to our own "reality." And because our own reality evolves over time, it seems that there is nothing constant and permanent in fairness. It is only a relative, subjective concept without any objective significance—a purely subjective illusion.

# Temporal

Our life can be compared to a project. Projects have a beginning and an end. Its definition states that it is not permanent—it has a definitive life span. It starts, goes on, and ends. A project has no purpose itself—it is only the means for something. It has a purpose and it is used as the vehicle, the tool, for the objective. Temporal is an interesting term. Something has an existence in time and, therefore, it has to have a starting point and moment as well as have an ending point and time. It is only temporal. Everything that exists in time has its own tempo, time, and place. Nothing is permanent.

Birth, living, and dying. Often the transition points are interesting. In those points, something changes from one formulation into another—a real drastic transformation happens. Still, our own life is mainly characterized by the middle part—the continuation. We focus almost no attention on the beginning or the end. For us, the living part is the only real existence and we ignore the beginning and the end. But how can we know what to do and where to go and, more importantly, where to target if we are not aware of all three characteristics—the beginning, the continuation, and the end—of temporal existence?

# What We Know

We are used to living surrounded by information. Our schools teach us the value of knowledge and details. TV is full of quizzes and competitions to test for cleverness. Education is emphasized everywhere we go. Each morning and evening, people learn the latest news. It is important to know what's happening and the topics of the day. But what do we really know?

Do we know what we know? Often we behave like we are very knowledgeable and have all the facts. Most of us are very keen on presenting our own points of view. We have opinions. Seldom do we consider whose opinions we are really repeating. Have we considered the items thoroughly and find arguments for and against the issue? Are we sure that our sources of information are objective and provide the complete picture? On what grounds is our thinking based?

Usually, we come to the conclusion that the more we investigate and study a subject, the less we know about it. Our thinking is based on a structure that needs to categorize and polarize items. We need straight and simple answers that are based on comparing and contrasting. We call this "putting things in relation to." There is a need to prefer and value something over something else. Otherwise we are said to be undecided. What happens when we are urged to set things into a relationship but we have limited knowledge and information?

Our ignorance results from our limited perception and understanding of issues. Also the need to value things (i.e., being able to "decide") creates a lot of confusion and misinterpretations. Therefore, what we know is less important than what we do not know. Unfortunately, most of the time our knowledge does not expand enough for us to realize that we do not know what we do not know. In other words, we may act with the best of intentions, but what is more arrogant than claiming to know something that we do not have a clue about?

What can we do so that we know as much as Socrates? Be humble. Humbleness rises from the knowledge and insight that we are not omnipotent and, therefore, cannot know very much of anything. We have to be sensitive and open-minded to realize this. The greatest minds in the world have claimed to know very little—how about us? What do we know?

# Trapped in a Box

*Within a shelter,*
*Covered in a case,*
*Limited by boundaries,*
*Extended by nature.*

*Trapped in the illusion,*
*Bewildered at times,*
*Lacking the courage,*
*Bravery, and persistence,*
*Of final breakthrough,*
*Transcending for the unknown.*

*The common is the bliss,*
*Misery, and sadness,*
*Of known and accepted,*
*Which horrific would be to lose,*
*And be replaced by something new.*

*To stretch the limits,*
*Ignore the lines,*
*Forget the known,*
*Unlearn the rest,*
*Exist in full,*
*Here and now,*
*Wake from the drowse.*

# Life and Death

# Life

*Life is a moment, a declara-*
*tion;*
*It puts us into a test,*
*of persistence and consistence;*
*It kindly teaches us the origin,*
*of who we are and what we*
*are.*

*Life keeps us busy,*
*Let us find our way.*
*It whispers in our ears,*
*and shows us the road.*
*The journey is long,*
*we have to do it alone;*
*Often we are lost,*
*and the road is gone.*
*We reach for guidance,*
*and struggle to stumble the*
*way.*

*The road is the way,*
*and the journey is the end;*
*Only choices are ours,*
*they accompany our way;*
*The trip is hard,*
*often uphill and more down-*
*hill;*
*heading forward seems so far*
*away.*

*Life is true;*
*it never lets us down.*
*Our mind is tricky,*
*it gives us a hard time.*
*We believe its lies,*
*sights of wit and fame.*
*We run to shortcuts,*
*and forget the way;*
*Life kindly leads us back,*
*but soon we head again our*
*way.*

*We never seem to learn,*
*but, therefore, life is the way.*

# Breathing

Life is breathing. It has three different phases—inhalation, short pause, and exhalation. Internal and external action—visible and invisible. Active and passive.

Breathing is living. Its intensity varies with scale. Some breathe faster than others—their perceptions and realizations are relative to their tempo. Small beings (e.g., cells) have different breathing cycles than large beings (with larger mass), such as humans, when compared to each other. Still, the relative cycle is intact. This can be realized only in cross-scale comparisons.

Life is a realization process (i.e., existence/manifestation) in time. In other words, life is relative motion where the subject's internal frame of reference is relational to its breathing cycle. A self-conscious being has the potential to experience various cycles at once (interlinked) and focus within a cycle in any of the three directions. The subjective intensity remains constant, but in relation to an external reference frame, significant relative time adjustments or movements can be experienced.

# Dailies

Actors monitor their performances by watching the dailies. The best dailies are watched by no one. We just live them.

We would learn so much by being able to watch our own dailies each evening. Weekly review, not even yearly or decadewide appraisal, would be sufficient. Most of the time we are so busy, so occupied with something to do.

The TV is on, the radio at least. If we have a free moment, we catch up on the unread papers or magazines. While we await the next meeting or appointment, we spend our few spare moments talking to someone on the cell phone. We have got nothing to do at home? Start cleaning. Arrange your record collection. Go for a coffee. Never stop. Fill your life with action and noise.

Feel important. Feel loved. Feel experienced. Feel busy. Feel balanced. Feel secure. Feel happy.

What happens if we stop? Can we stop? Most of our lives we are hiding, escaping, filling the blanks by occupying ourselves. Refusing to face ourself. We look for easy fixes.

We're after feeling good. We're after happiness. The problem is that our perception of happiness changes the minute we achieve what we were after. Our object of desire and happiness shifts from item to item, never stopping. We're like hamsters in the wheel—until we decide to step out of it. To do that, we need to see the dailies first. Not many of us have found those. They are hidden to the world we know nothing about. They are too close to us. We just live them by spinning the wheel.

# Flow of Time

Flow of time is an illusion. Time is motion. It has a duration—a measurement of motion from one point to another. Quantum mechanics do not behave this way and, therefore, Einstein was more than a bit upset: "God does not play dice with the universe."

The paradox is that we are always in motion—if not physically at least in our mind. We are never really in the moment. Our mind wanders around endlessly either recalling past memories and experiences or projecting things for the future. Our mind reacts for the current moment while not being able to experience the current now time as it is. We do not see the world as it is. Our own view of the world is adjusted and biased, depending on our personal history, cultural background, social and behavioral standards and expectations, as well as experience and memories of similar situations in the past. We see what we know, and we know what we have experienced in the past. See the loop?

We crave security and predictability. We want to have stability in our lives. Unfortunately, "now" is always new—unknown. It is a dynamic process that cannot be known beforehand. It destroys part of the known in order to create something new. Therefore it is called the "change." Still, we want to be able to be in control. We cannot stand the unpredictable—at least our mind thinks so.

Have you tried to keep your mind still, not thinking about the future or the past? Not thinking about anything while walking in the street. Purely observing and appreciating whatever comes your way. What happens? By not letting your mind label and judge things around you and squeezing your observations into a historical framework (your experience or prejudice), you start to see clearly and register more than ever about the world around you. And the best part is that you can even recall those things later on. You can visualize your entire route to work or home, with all the details and passersby, not even talking about their clothing or what they were saying and so on. All this is possible because your mind is not "working," thinking about the past or worrying about the future. You're free to live in the moment—always in the timeless now time.

How could you know something beforehand and label it because the now moment is ever changing, new all the time, the unknown? Still our static mind wants to control something dynamic. And it always fails, but we do not see it. Our mind has its tricks to hide its own faults. It lays blame in all the other directions. It's always somebody else's fault. Our expectations are not fulfilled. We are sad or angry, frustrated or surprised, thanks to our mind. But who created those expectations and thoughts in the first place? They did not happen, as the physical world exists, objectively. They were our own mind's creations, which we treated as real. They became real for us. They are our own "static" creation, which did not align with the real world—the now time.

It's time to stop extrapolating the past for the current moment and take life as it comes. Without objections or force. Just by letting go and letting it flow.

# The Framework

Our culture, society, administration, political system, infrastructure, laws, processes, properties, possessions, and even money are just a framework. They are the setting, the means for the essence. These things change and evolve over time. Technology develops and we gain more knowledge and understanding, which is reflected in the world around us. Our collective knowledge changes through the decades and centuries. We call this development.

Still, a framework is not the essence. It only provides the raw material and the tools for the real action. It is easy to get confused with means and objectives along the road. The framework is not important even though it surrounds us. We need it but we should not get carried away by it.

The framework does not define who we are—it can only state what we have. Our real reference frame is not vis-à-vis the framework but relates to other living beings. How we treat others describes who we are. We cannot live in isolation and solely with the framework, we need the real point of reference that defines us. The essential things are universal and eternal. They are not dependent on the development of the framework or any particular condition or point in time in the framework. Throughout the centuries, the writings and advice about personal ethics and integrity have stayed the same in essence. They describe the issues about how to live together and in relation to other living things—despite the circumstances.

Our surroundings enable us to declare who we are. The framework sets us into different situations and positions. Sometimes life is hard and at other moments it is something else. The essence is that no matter the circumstances, we should still be the same—the person we declare ourself to be.

Because how can we say we are one way when the circumstances are in our favor and yet appear as something else when
they are no longer ideal? We should be able to be who we are
in all cases and at all times—no matter what happens. We
should be like the rock solid ground that stays put in a storm
as well as in the sunshine and on a beautiful summer day. The
framework makes it possible for us to define and declare who
we are—despite what we have or how we are.

Our challenge is to concentrate on the essence and use the
framework as our means to declare who we are. We do this by
living in the framework and for every moment, stating by our
actions our real nature. The way we treat all other people, who
are facing different circumstances and situations than us, is
the real test onto which we should focus our energies, 24/7.
So, who you are (in relation to other people) and on which
issues have you been focusing today?

# Illusion of a Free Will

We're free to do whatever we desire. We have a free will—or do we?

How free is our will? Are we able to decide what are we going to do tomorrow? We can plan things but we cannot always guarantee that things are going to turn out the way we have planned. Other things can happen. So where is the free will?

Even if we forget the future and just focus on our behavior I'm not sure that we have any freedom at all. Pick a situation that could happen in your life. How do you think you will behave? What kind of decisions do you think you will make in this situation?

For example, you're in a traffic jam and already late for a meeting. No big deal. You have been in the situation before. How do you act? Do you behave differently every time? Most likely not. You just follow the pattern or habit you have mechanically repeated time after time. You react. Even if the situation is a brand new one for you, you still have an idea of how you will act in the moment when it happens. We are stuck with our own thinking and perceptions of the world. We are dragging our past with us, and it ties us to the behavior patterns and sets the limits to our freedom of choices. How free is a will that cannot innovate and create new dynamic responses every moment? Repeating old formulas does not sound so free after all. Couples who have been together for a long time know what each other will say or do beforehand—each has learned the other partner's thinking pattern. Very original and free, indeed.

Free will is an illusion. From the outset, it looks like everything is possible. By observing the issue more carefully, though, we start to realize that the true freedom of will is mainly limited to our point of view (perception)—how we take the events that occur in our lives. Are we sad, disappointed, angry, frustrated, and so forth?

Next time you're late for a meeting and traffic is really jammed, instead of getting red and speeding around, try catching yourself in the middle of getting angry and just change your behavior. No point getting angry—you're already late. You cannot reverse the clock. Why not be in a good mood and instead enjoy the ride. This will be less stressful, and you might even avoid a ticket. Sounds more free to me. The trick is to keep this new perception going—all the time. Don't follow the old thinking formulas every moment—be awake. If you do this, you might even do something unpredictable, fresh.

# Life

Do we know what it is to live? We say we're living. So we should be masters of life. What does it mean to be alive?

It looks like a lot of routines and useless everyday tasks. We call it the ordinary life. But by being alive we mean none of those moments of gray days and sleepy mornings. For us to be alive is about experiences and moments that stick out from the ordinary—something to remember, no matter whether it was for good or bad. Nietzsche wrote about his own life and marked that his weakest moments were his greatest moments. They made him stronger.

Our greatest moments are the ones where we have experienced something meaningful. They have taught us something about life, about its sadness, sorrow, beauty, joy, anger, hatred, love, happiness, or freedom. These lessons usually do not come easily. Many times it means that we have to break out of the ordinary, safe life, and we can be caught by surprise. Experiences require us to extend our limits—come out of our safety zone. (Otherwise they would be part of our ordinary lives.) Sometimes stretches are giant leaps that hurt us deeply.

On the other hand, some experiences happen out of nowhere, where we can just enjoy the beautiful moment with total harmony like a sunset on a perfect summer day. There are no expectations, and we take life as it comes, with no fear or stress but just with curiosity and open-mindedness—like in a holiday trip.

What are the moments you're the most proud of? For many, these moments are ones where we have done something that we believe was the "right thing to do." Something noble, humble, unselfish—almost heroic. We were not thinking about ourselves, we were acting for a greater good. Hollywood movies, fairytales, and novels are full of these stories. They resonate in us and give us a good feeling. Somehow it's built on us and is universal. Is that to be truly alive and the purpose of life? Or is it called love? And what if love, life, and truth are just different names for the same purpose, and our journey is to get to know them by living and experiencing.

# Resistance

You can see it from the outset. Some people have lots of worries and they have a large weight on their shoulders; they are almost buried under the burden. Most of us, however, are somewhere in between. We have some concerns and troubles that create stress and tension, but we manage with them. Still, we cannot say that we are entirely free as a bird and independent of any worries. Why is that?

Our life is like a freely flowing river. It has a tremendous energy but while it can flow without any obstacles, we cannot feel the power. Every one of us has the same amount of energy in us. What makes us different is the way we use this energy. If we just let it flow without any obstacles, things are easy and there are no worries. We are happy and free of any burdens. We can do tremendous things and share the happiness with other people as well. We radiate and people love to be around us. For a few, this is the case. The rest of us block our energy flow and create bigger or smaller obstacles for ourselves. These barriers are like a dam. It requires static energy to keep the water blocked. But when the current gets too strong, the dam gives way.

Our own resistance and denial create these dams. We want to be in control and turn our life in the direction we desire; we refuse to live life as it happens. Or even better, we would like our life to stay still. Our internal dams are the ones that create the tension and the bad feelings in us. The greater the disruption, the bigger the amount of energy required to keep things status quo. This is the burden we feel on our shoulders. Sometimes our worries are so big that they start to fill our entire life. We are really depressed. We are disappointed in our life. Life has not turned out the way we planned it. Finally, we accept the new situation and move on. We destroy the dam and let life flow again. We feel free and anything is possible—for a small while. Then we start to resist again with small incremental steps.

If we realize that resistance does not solve anything, it only postpones the inevitable, we could jump out of the cycle. By purely accepting the undeniable flow of life without any predictability, we can set ourselves free. We do not have to resist. We can just let go and take every moment as it comes—without any expectations or reservations. When there is nothing to wait for, there is nothing to be disappointed in either. No surprises. Nothing to stress about. No tension or discomfort. Only pure living, with the rich variety of entirely new moments and possibilities every moment.

# Time Travel

It's funny that we desire to travel through time. Besides self-ish interest, what purpose would it serve? We are actually time travelers all the time. Or should I say channel surfers?

We get carried away either by thinking about our past or piling up with dreams of the future. These two activities take most of our time. The actual now moment we are currently experiencing is something we would rather not like to have. It's far better and safer to sail in our dreams, where all the outcomes are already known and we can speculate with endless what-if scenarios. The future is even better. For us it has not happened yet and, therefore, we can make it up any way we desire. Well, almost. The only limitation is that we cannot just dream about anything of which we have no knowledge. For example, in medieval times people did not dream about having cars and flying around the world in airplanes. So dreaming is also quite boring. All the outcomes are predictable in one way or another—like LEGO blocks that can only be set up in a certain way based on their shapes.

Our channel surfing concerns the current living moment. We seldom stay in the channel. We'd rather jump on and off many times in a second. This happens by switching either to the dream or the history channel. Reality TV is something we prefer to consume as a recorded version, just to be on the safe side.

Still, all the action happens in the reality mode. We cannot change our history and cannot predict the future. We have to do all the things right now. The paradox is that the only unpredictable (and therefore nonboring) moment is the fresh now time, what we are all the time experiencing. And the best part is that it's interactive. We can take part in all the activities and get involved. It's amazing how many of us are not taking up this opportunity. People would rather switch to old classics or sci-fi stories that have predictable endings. They'd rather opt for something that smells, tastes, and sounds like real life but is not. Artificial life seems to be the best act in town.

Considering the low ratings for actually living in the moment, it is amazing that people would even dream of time traveling. What would they do then if they cannot live now? Sure it's a more interactive TV show to go for the future and know that you are able to come back to the original time whenever things start to get too serious (or should I say real?). Time travel would be just another way of surfing channels— just a sportier version compared to staring at a glass box or daydreaming from the sofa.

Nevertheless, the basic fact is that we always figure out new ways to escape reality. We'd rather either skip to our own natural channels or use the manmade "entertainment" options. When was the last time you really watched some-thing on the TV or listened to the radio? Most of the time, we are desperate to fill up any silent moments by whatever back-ground noise from TV, radio, or MP3 players we can find. Still, the fact is that you cannot avoid living in the moment— you can only pretend you're not there. How good our skills are determine how good our private scam is. Our consciousness is always on, and it is permanently stuck on the reality channel. And most of us just cannot live without constantly surfing channels. Restless 24/7 escape from the reality—out now!

# When?

Time is a great paradox. We are almost never in the time. Being in the moment is almost nonexistent for us. When do we have the time?

Time is a concept that has many purposes for us. It enables us to escape from the current moment. We can either wander around our past or dream about the future, but still we have to perform all these activities in the now time. Sometimes time is precious for us. At other times, we are bored and cannot wait to skip the moment. Why does time sometimes fly and at other times crawl?

It seems that we are so busy trying to do something in the future or worrying about the past that we simply do not have "time" for the moment. Why do we always have to do something—can we not just enjoy the moment and take the future as it comes? How many of us can plan the future and then implement it as we have figured it out? Is there any bigger waste of time than worrying or dreaming about things that might occur but most likely will not happen the way we have planned?

Usually we would prefer to be anywhere but where we are. This applies to being in the moment as well. We always have to achieve or gain something. And for those things, we need time. There is never enough time to do all the things we can imagine. But do we really have to use all our energy to be like zombies who are not much present in the current moment?

Only a few human beings can live in the moment. It is easy to notice these people; they are very intense and present in the moment. One can get their undivided attention and their presence is often very penetrating. They are more focused—they purely are, fully. Being able to keep this state every minute, hour, and time of the day requires practice. It means that we are not busy to worry about the past or plan the future. We concentrate on every moment as it comes and appreciate it as if it were to be our last one. And how do you know that this is not your final day of existence? Would you use the time some other way than the way you are using it right now? The challenge is to live every moment as if it is all we have left. This way, there is no time to be wasted—we only experience and live intensively.

# Death

In our language death means the opposite of living. Being alive is to live, create, explore, and experience. Death is something where nothing is moving and everything stays still, a total freeze or a complete stop. It is something where nothing new is developed nor does anything change; death is simply a state where nothing is created anymore.

In order to be truly alive, one should be familiar with death. What does it mean not to be alive? Not to create, explore, and experience? Stay still, hold back, freeze the situation, and maintain the status quo? Resist movement or change?

How can we be sure that we are not already dead? To put it differently, are we really experiencing, continuously creating and exploring something new? We are not eager to explore and break the boundaries. We are not so excited about anything new and unknown happening. We'd rather not rock the boat and stay still and lie low. We are uncomfortable with change and prefer the current situation, no matter how bad or awkward.

Change happens very slowly in the physical world. Drastic renewal takes decades or generations rather than weeks or years. Our mind is quick to draw scenarios and imagine things, but real implementation of visible action takes decades, if not centuries. We drag our history with us. We are conservative and changing only with force. Someone who does something only when under external pressure is not creating. Where is the freedom and joy of exploration? To put it in brief—we are dead.

# Death and Dying

Have you ever considered what dying means? Often we are very shady and quiet about death. It is something we do not want to consider or think about. It is a taboo. It is something that only happens to somebody else—not to us. In other words—we are afraid of it. But why?

What exactly are we afraid of? Something we do not know anything about? Maybe.

Dying means that we are departed instantly from everything we are attached to and have. We have to give away everything so familiar and "natural" to us, something and everything we have taken for granted. Our health, physical body, friends, family, wealth, possessions, lifestyle, habits, and so on. This is death. It is detachment.

Clinging and attachment do not have to be physical in nature. We can have obsessions, desires, needs, and cravings. Suddenly we cannot satisfy those by physical means anymore. We are forced to be without them. This is death.

We have to die in order to live. What does that mean? We think that we are alive and kicking when we are driven by our lower qualities like desire, lust, obsession, and so on. Satisfying and fulfilling these consume most of our lives. We call this living. We are in a never-ending circle where old needs are fulfilled and instantly new ones arise. How liberating and happy!

Being truly alive means that we are free to live, not obsessed or forced continuously to fulfil something. Free to be. In order to achieve this, we have to set ourselves free from our attachments and desires. They are strong and we cannot win them by force. The more we resist them, the larger they become. We can beat them only by ignoring them, by learning to live without them, by detaching ourselves from everything in a similar manner—as death will do to us, finally, but this time we do it voluntarily, gradually.

It is a misunderstanding to believe that detachment will mean literally dying and living without anything interesting or fun. On the contrary, how much fun and freedom do you have when you are obsessed by something? Detachment does not mean giving up living—only giving away all the attachment and clinging. You can still enjoy the sunrise and have a delicious meal, but the difference is that those do not bear any utility value for you anymore—they simply are. There is no need for anything. One is not lacking anything because need implicitly declares a lack of something (i.e., the object of the need).

Clinging and attachment are based on ignorance, and de facto the only thing to give away is the wrong understanding. Greater wisdom liberates. Always.

# Give Away

*The more we let go,*
*the more we gain,*
*right choices,*
*and confidence;*

*Knowing the way,*
*gives us the lead,*
*the bearing and the heading,*
*that guide us through,*
*the storms and thunders,*
*sunshine and rains,*
*through the gates,*
*of rose gardens and caves;*

*Our way,*
*is not here to stay,*
*it provides us,*
*the illusion of power,*
*control and sorrow;*
*It gives us the taste,*
*but lets us down;*
*Or is it us,*
*thinking of great achieve-*
*ments,*
*of our deeds when things turn,*
*our way thanks to luck,*
*or by other cause,*
*hidden the truth,*
*is from us?*

*Therefore easy for us to claim,*
*victory and gain,*
*but hard to admit the case,*
*where nothing from us,*
*helped to prevent,*
*a single item,*
*where everything went,*
*the other way,*
*we never anticipated,*
*or expected to gain.*

*Many years,*
*more decades,*
*lots of times,*
*we repeat our way,*
*control and sorrow,*
*illusion of gain,*
*where all the good,*
*is of ours;*
*Opposite results,*
*caused by others,*
*how strange it is,*
*when picking up the cherries,*
*from the cake,*
*is the way we hide away;*
*Give away,*
*let it go, all the way,*
*let if flow;*
*No control, no gain,*

*no sorrow, no pain,*
*no future, no past,*
*only here,*
*experiencing to last;*
*Easier way,*
*no stress to strain,*
*only the wise,*
*realize this,*
*the others try,*
*till they fail.*
*Give away,*
*no other way.*

# Mind

# Thought

*Suffering or joy,*
*quest or rest,*
*happiness or agony,*
*together or alone,*
*now or then,*
*you or me,*
*here or there,*
*sun or moon,*
*sand or sea,*
*one plus one,*
*music or art,*
*history or novel,*
*writing or verbal,*
*all the same,*
*underneath,*
*different by appearance,*
*disguised for the most,*
*of their genuine nature,*
*pure and simple,*
*of a thought;*

*Nevertheless,*
*varies with persistence,*
*but follows the same,*
*pattern of,*
*coming,*
*sustaining,*
*and going;*

*Always afresh,*
*never the same,*
*appearance may stay,*
*but no thing is the same;*

*Deep thought,*
*shallow dream,*
*clear and sharp,*
*vague and soft,*
*fragile or strong,*
*short or long,*
*still the same,*
*real for the one,*
*illusion for the second,*
*relative for both,*
*ideas, all the same.*

# Forms

Our world is based on dualities comprising items in time and space. In other words, our life happens by and around physical concepts and things. This material preference is prevailing and very carefully reflected in our mind as well.

All the important issues are formless. Joy, happiness, wisdom, knowledge, beauty, and love, to name a few. Plato introduced us to the ancient wisdom of forms or ideas. He spoke about pure ideal concepts that are perfect. For example, an ideal concept of horse is something that is never entirely captured in the physical horses. Still, we can realize the ideal concept of a horse by observing the variety of horses around us.

How do we think? We create images. These conceptual items are not from the ideal world but consist of our experiences. We can reconstruct something that we already know. Our mind is used to creating physical forms. What happens when we try to squeeze a formless concept into a material existence?

It is the same as taking a photo—a snapshot of real life. A photo is never the real thing. It does not smell or taste or cannot be by any means compared to the real thing. Still, this is the way our mind works. It takes snapshots over and over again and tries to imitate the formless and eternal, perfect, concepts. We chase these ideas by using physical things and items as if they were the formless perfect concepts. Our mind transfers the ideal concepts into physical objects and does its best to give us the illusion of the real thing. And we are lured—all the way. But every time we have "consumed" these mind creations, we are not satisfied. We realize that they are not the entire truth. We long for the real thing—and off we go again.

The puzzle can be solved the same way as Plato's famous *The Allegory of the Cave*. One has to realize the real thing and break free from the chains. We have to set ourselves free from our mind and its creations. As long as we continue putting forms to something that cannot have a form, we are living in an imperfect world, which makes us crave the original concepts.

Formless items cannot be captured in time and space. They have to be experienced instantly. Over and over again. They do not bend to the physical existence. They are the real thing, forever and right now.

# Compromised Dumpster

We are in the garbage-creation business. The products and results are our own creation, and the consequences are observable around the world. Most of the garbage is all in our own mind. The dumpster in question is not a physical one in its original form—its derivations can be, however. This huge dumpster is called our mind. It's the creator and initiator of all the garbage. Simply, that is its pure existence and raison d´être. How does this polluter work?

We live only in the moment—now time. Nothing else is available to us. Nevertheless, we can do various things with this now time but still everything happens in the moment. For example, we can think back through our memories and reflect on everything that has happened. We can also project the future and wonder or worry about the next moments. Still, all of these actions are happening in the moment. Our sole decision is just how to use every moment. We can either concentrate on the moment or opt for escaping from the reality, either to our past or into the projected future our mind creates for us.

There would not be any dumpster if we always live in the moment. We would take life as it comes and make the necessary decision as is required. Very simple, no worries at all. Things just happen, and life would be only the issues that emerge to us, some good and some less desirable—all the same because we can only take them as they come.

The above is unfortunately not the way we live. We prefer to be in "control." Therefore, we have to know what happens next. Otherwise we could not have this control illusion. How much control do you have if you cannot predict the future outcomes? Well, this is exactly the paradox. In practice, we are not in control, but we believe we are. Our way of living is based on the trick our mind plays on us. And the results are the huge dumpster we are dragging behind us.

Our mind knows only what we know. It is limited to its own boundaries and it is not objective where we are concerned. It cannot exist without us. We produce the mind. Therefore, it is also the one who creates for us the future—the illusion of time in the moment. The mind works very simply: It fabricates the future from our personal experiences and knowledge. In other words, it extrapolates the past and the current moment to the future based on its previous knowledge. It's very logical and nice; it's also very real and acceptable to us—after all, it's a familiar future to us. We have created it and can understand it. It is easy to accept and fall in love with. How can we not like our own creation?

Our mind provides us with illusions of the future that we take for granted and as true to us. These snapshots create different kinds of feelings, emotions, and sensations in us. The mind projects usually either good or bad outcomes. The previous we dream about and the latter we are scared of or worried about. These outcomes cause new feelings, and the snapshots or pictures start to have existences of their own. They can also create new outcomes and sensations in us. Often, the outcome is that we cling to these illusions and feelings that arise in us. We forget the actual projected route to the future moment and see only the "prediction of the future." Now it's true to us. We are sure it is going to happen, no doubt about it. It must happen. How horrible or how wonderful.

This is the moment when we produce the garbage. After seeing the beautiful outcome we cling to it. This is something we definitely need or want. Yes, no doubt about it. We are urged to direct our actions toward this outcome. At the moment we are not yet there but for us it is possible because it seems so real for us, thanks to our mind. Now we have two different points to compare: the current moment and the projected future outcome. An urge or desire has been aroused in us. Now we know what we want. This can happen in various of forms: greed, anger, frustration, jealousy, self-justification, and so on, depending on our projection and the gap between the now time and the imagined future. From this point onward, we live in the moment only in a manner that is directed and geared toward the outcome we illusioned. In other words, we have accepted the future our mind projected and are compromising in our principles and behavior in order to make sure that the future will happen the way we desired it to occur.

You still remember how all this started? Our mind fabricated a future for us based on the experiences and knowledge we have at the moment. It did not have any capabilities to provide us any directions or predictions of the actual reality that will emerge. Still, we believed the nice or horrible scenario it provided us with and now we are living like if these illusions are as sure things as our past memories. The compromised garbage is all the things we produced in our mind and now desire. These compromise and corrupt our behavior and actions in the now time. Our mind offered us this great future picture and catered the table with good reasons and justifications to make it happen.

We no longer observe the world as it emerges. We observe and see the world only through the lenses our mind produced for us. We expect our projections to happen. Disappointments and regret emerge from the realization that the future occurred some other way than we expected. We are not in control. We could have even given up and sacrificed some of our humble and noble principles in our quest to perceive and "force" the illusioned reality to happen.

The compromised dumpster accumulates and reminds us, thanks to our mind. It accumulates these memories and fabricates more future outcomes. More garbage coming in—until we catch the litter itself and get rid of it, just ignore it totally. We give up our very mind and start living with mindlessness in the moment. We take life as it emerges and base our actions on the reality as it comes. What a fresh and pure existence!

# Mindlessness

*"When you talk, you only say something that you already know; when you listen, you learn what someone else knows."*—Anonymous.

This quote applies to our mind as well. Usually we are busy thinking and processing something. Our mind is like a railway station—thoughts coming or going at all times. Actually they cannot stop. They only come and go. If we are packed with existing concepts and ideas, how could we expect to get new ideas and experience something fresh?

Mindlessness is a state where our mind keeps still. It is not a passive state. On the contrary; it is a state where we are active and receptive to something new. Mindlessness is about clearing the mind from old thoughts and concepts and making space for something unknown and fresh. The unknown does not come with loud noise and force. It is a quiet visitor that avoids brutal action. It makes room for more harsh forms. Therefore, one cannot order it to come—it comes when it is appropriate for it to appear. Mindlessness is a dynamic state that happens in now time. It cannot be stored or reproduced for further usage. It cannot be restored. We have to come to it—to prepare ourselves for it.

# Planning

When are we very positively surprised and overwhelmed? When something out of the ordinary and unexpected happens, something we have not thought about—something fresh and new to us. This happens outside of our (previous) experience and knowledge, and it makes us happy and joyful. We would love to be more spontaneous, but it is so hard and difficult. Why?

We love to plan things. It is great to think ahead and imagine the details and occasions we want to accomplish and live by. Planning is something we do naturally. Most of it is done purely for practical reasons and for everyday routines. We need to schedule and arrange our life in a way so we can take care of our obligations and duties. Worrying is a special type of planning—it concentrates on the negative issues and their potential occurrences. We are not actually "planning" for an occurrence, but being afraid and speculating about all the possible outcomes and issues that could happen. A positive type of planning is dreaming. We dream about great things that we would like to achieve and gain, moments and experiences that we think would make us happy. Nevertheless, all of this is just our mind game. Some of it is practical and necessary, but most of it is a total waste of energy and effort. Actually, it can prevent us from experiencing more and greater things than we are ever capable of dreaming (or planning) about.

Our plans are derived from our experience and knowledge. They project the future as we can imagine it. This makes the future predictable and "ordinary" for us. We can imagine it and dream about it—live it in our mind beforehand. It cannot include anything that we cannot know about. Certainly it has nothing to do with the reality. We have no means to plan the future. Still, planning often makes our life "boring." And it makes it feel like every day is the same and repeats the same patterns over and over again. No day is any different, and nothing new happens. Sound familiar?

When we plan things, we are preparing to live according to our plan, which means that we are not open for the moment or anything new. We live according to our already thought through plan, merely executing and implementing that plan. Like robots that "think" what happens next and follow the preprogrammed plan, we do not actually live in the moment. This makes life boring and predictable. We "hypnotize" and make ourselves believe our plan, and then we see and hear what we want to hear and see—according to our own manuscript—we create a catch-22. How can we experience something new if we always live according to our existing knowledge?

Sometimes we run into an interesting person or do something crazy. These are the times when we live in the moment. We are not planning but experiencing and letting life carry us forward. Life offers us many great surprises and opportunities every day, but we have to be awake and ready to acknowledge them. Often we appear too busy or occupied to carry out the daily activities we have planned and expected to accomplish everything. But it is too scary not to plan. It implicitly tells us that we might not be in control, something we prefer not to experience. We would rather plan and know what to expect. It is safer this way, even though often our mind creates the misery and sadness because we are too afraid to welcome something new. It is the unknown we are so scared of, that which we cannot plan for or know beforehand.

This is the great step we have to take. Once we make it over the threshold, we realize that all the worrying was for nothing. Life actually becomes more interesting and exciting when we are open for the opportunities. Plans are unnecessary because life often turns out differently than how we had imagined it. Being free and living in the moment give us a tremendous amount of energy to experience and observe because we are not tied up in planning for the future. Reality is an even better planner than we are; it is the only thing that can give us positive surprises. We cannot plan our own joy and happiness—and we are even less capable of planning to surprise ourselves! Plan less and experience more. Is that a plan?

# Predetermined Life

We want to be in control. We are not comfortable with unpredictability. We would prefer to live in a predictable, ordinary way, without any surprises. This is the underlying assumption in our behavior.

Predictable, controllable life, however, is an oxymoron. We hate to change, but on the other hand we long for excitement and thrills. We want to be positively surprised and experience something new and unknown. The ordinary life is a routine we do not like either, and we would prefer to get some excitement, but we want to choose when and the way it occurs—nothing too extreme and yet still new for us.

Sounds quite complicated? No, it is totally the opposite. Simply, we are just bored and scared to death. We want to cling to our perceptions of the world but still get some amusement when we have had enough of all the sameness. In other words, we like to live in our own well-thought-out world with all the nitty-gritty details and relations in nice little boxes and labels we have defined and predetermined.

Occasionally, we tire of the predetermined perception of the world and want a peek at the reality. But we do not want to see too much. It might destroy our sense of security and the wonderland we have formed in our mind. We are scared and out of balance when we cannot explain and understand something new or strange. This is especially the case with negative issues that happen in our life, whereas positive surprises are always welcome. We actually would prefer to get them almost all the time.

I must say that we are quite interesting creatures. We want to live in our own small sandboxes without any disturbance. Each person is the king of the hill, as long as he or she does not have to step down from his or her place on the hill and face the real world—the great unknown and the stage of all plays.

# Questions for Self-Inquiry

Where do our feelings and thoughts arise, appear, and vanish? There must be something that is not in movement in order to become aware of these states.

We experience time (i.e., past, present, and future) but how is it possible that we can become aware of these if we are a part of them (i.e., the observer would be part of the observation)?

Where is that continuous self-awareness (i.e., I am) that is ever present?

How is it possible to do self-inquiries for ourself? That means that the observer is observing himself or herself (e.g., an eye trying to look at itself).

Why can we change but our awareness of ourselves stays?

We build our world from five external senses—what is it like with more senses?

# Significance and Self

Who did you meet today? What did you see? Usually we answer these questions by mentioning the most significant incidents of the day.

When we are out walking, we meet many people but only a few of them, if any, do we remember later on. The same applies with all the details and items on our way. Why do we not register most of the activities and items? Why do we "see" only a fraction of the whole picture?

The most fascinating point is to realize that by getting a reaction we have already stated something. If there were no "self," it would mean that all the occurrences would be indifferent. There would not be any better or worse incidents—they would all be the same. But everyone gets different reactions from the same (or different) occurrences (i.e., impulses, actions, events, and so on). They bear a meaning for the self, and only for the self. Objectively, nothing bears any meaning. Things just are, like a rock or bird. No statements at all—just pure existence.

Having reactions or feelings proves that there is a self, something that sets relative values for impulses it receives. This insight clarified, at least for me, the point of selfness. For example, when a human being looks at you and intends to approach you, he or she has defined some significance to you that is stated by his or her actions. The opposite happens when you are totally ignored or ignore others. We just do not see most of the people at all while we are out walking. They neither exist nor bear any significance for us.

How about those people who register most of the actions and details around themselves but lay no significance to the occurrences. (Don't confuse these people with those discussed previously who do not "see" most of the world around them.)

This is the state of being selfless. They recognize and are aware of the things around them, but these items do not resonate (i.e., bear any significance) anything for the person. This is existence in its purest form. And in this state, we are able to recall the details and events later on. So it is not a passive state like the "blind" case in which a person does not recognize or see things around him or her. This situation can be verified by asking the person to recall the incident.

So, we are selfish as long as we have significant things in our lives. And this means that we have to bear the consequences as well. When one is selfless, there is nothing that is interfered or reacted to. And when there is no action, a reaction is not created either. Then our existence is very rich and instant—and more meaningful than ever before.

# Silence

Seldom can we experience silence by chance anymore. Walkmans, TVs, radio, traffic, and household appliances keep us company. There isn't any moment in a day when we would feel the silence without active effort. It takes a power blackout to get us even close to the silence. What is it like, the sound of silence?

We fill our life with action. Motion is important; destination and purpose are secondary. This is the case with silence as well. We regard it as something unnatural. We are afraid of the silence—the emptiness. It feels like something is missing or something is not right.

What happens when we are totally silent? By silence I mean internal silence—our mind is at rest. Naturally it helps if there are no external noises either. But when we are focused, the outside voices disappear to the background. Silence is an opportunity; it is a chance to experience something new. We can start to hear the sound of silence. By removing all the motion and noise one sets the mind free for something else to emerge.

Silence can teach us and let us experience something new. When we experience it more deeply, we start to realize that emptiness and silence are not totally without anything. Actually, they are the opposite. But we have to be open-minded and humble to experience the sound of silence.

# Memory

*Goes back only a short while,*
*forgets,*
*ignores,*
*leaves blank,*
*the things we did,*
*and are not proud about;*

*All the experiences,*
*of misery,*
*darkness,*
*abuse,*
*hate,*
*fear,*
*and betrayal,*
*we have not committed,*
*if you ask from your memory;*

*Still something in you,*
*reminds,*
*and remembers.*
*It tries to give you,*
*hints,*
*tips,*
*and kind notes,*
*but often we leave,*
*those without a blink,*
*turn the blind eye,*
*and hide away;*

*Opportunities come,*
*and go,*
*to settle the accounts,*

*straight,*
*leave our mark,*
*and balance the past;*

*Persistence of memory,*
*hidden deep,*
*and hard,*
*not easy by far,*
*is to bring into sunshine,*
*the old dusty,*
*deeds,*
*we rather would,*
*leave and bury deep;*

*Our memory is short,*
*and not for trusted,*
*feelings and the body,*
*better guides,*
*for the light and*
*the record straight;*

*Do not waste time,*
*to settle the accounts;*
*Your feelings lead,*
*to the deep mines,*
*of your secrets,*
*and sides,*
*way back,*
*far away,*
*you should stay*
*—awake.*

# Meditation

# When We Are

*When does all this suffering end?*
  *When we only are.*

*All this achieving and doing, is it ever enough?*
  *When we only are.*

*I'm trying to find happiness and joy in life—how can I succeed?*
  *When we only are.*

*How to cherish every moment?*
  *When we only are.*

*Is there a way to help other people in this crazy world?*
  *When we only are.*

*What is the opposite of doing and performing?*
  *When we only are.*

*How to reach a pure existence?*
  *When we are ready—we already are.*

# Concentration

Our life is hectic. Even more, our mind is restlessly moving. Our inner state is often noticeable for outsiders as well. When we are nervous or have difficulty being calm, this is reflected in our behavior. We move around, change position, look around, do our typical gestures, or otherwise keep in motion. All of these are just reflections of our inner perpetual mover—our mind. In other words, we have a very short concentration span. Therefore, thinking is also very difficult. It requires us to focus on one particular aspect and keep our mind fixed on the item we are processing.

Concentration can be taught. We can train our mind to become more controllable and under our will. Better concentration enables us to perform our daily life better, thus helping us to learn better and faster. We can observe, analyze, and perceive more clearly. Being able to focus on one thing at a time means that our effort can be directed to the very item we are dealing with and all our capacity is dedicated to the task at hand. Reading a book or listening to a lecture is easier if we are not distracted by other thoughts or surrounding stimuli. A distracted mind can be compared to a light bulb. It radiates in all directions and, therefore, loses its illuminative power, thanks to a lack of focus. A concentrated mind is like a laser beam; it is very precise and powerful.

Clear and precise thoughts require a concentrated mind. Good speech or articulation is based on focused effort and well-prepared concepts. Concentration helps us communicate and be better understood. But how do we accomplish it?

We need practice. And even more patience. One cannot become masters overnight. Our mind requires continuous exercise and training. This can be done at various levels, but the good thing is that almost no matter what we do we can turn it into a concentration practice. An easy start is to stop doing many things at once. Turn off the radio if you're writing or checking your e-mail. Or listen to the radio, but don't do anything else—perform only one task at a time.

Training our memory is as important as improving our concentration. Our mind and concentration are interlinked. Stop making shopping lists and use your memory instead. Also, when you catch your mind wandering from the topic you're thinking about, try to trace back your route to discover how you got distracted. Acknowledge at every moment what you're doing. If you are walking or driving, concentrate on doing this task. Gradually, you will become better and more concentrated without an effort. By fragmenting our concentration, we do many things poorly. Top artists and athletes need total concentration to be successful—and they practice a lot. Why shouldn't we?

# Detachment

We often get carried away or overwhelmed by our emotions. We call this a state of being emotional or sometimes even irrational. In practice, we mean that we were in a condition where we were vulnerable to act in a way in which we might not normally act (i.e., we regret our behavior later on). In other words, we are stating that we lost control of ourselves; we were not "we" in the ordinary sense.

Detachment is a state of being where one observes everything from a distance. This means that one is not getting carried away or being emotionally more or less out of control (i.e., getting angry and so on). Detachment does not mean that we are passive or not involved in the moment—totally the opposite. It means that we are capable of being observant and active in every moment and, therefore, a more precise perception and behavior in life is possible.

Detachment is not dependent on the situation. It does not matter whether we are experiencing joyful and happy moments or sad and unpleasant surprises. Keeping a small distance from all matters enables us to have broader understanding of the issues and circumstances. Our personal ego and interests cannot block our way. Actually one learns to identify those, and in time gets rid of any personal selfish motives. No more big mood swings to the negative or positive—we can purely experience life as it comes without our expectations getting in our way. A fresh way of living.

# Enlightenment

Meditation is preparation for the continuous steady state of enlightenment, a process where one is adjusting to shift the consciousness onto a higher level. Doing this requires concentration and undivided attention. Still, we cannot progress by physical "force" or pure power of will. We have to reach a higher (or finer) state where we are capable of oscillating the energy state that enables the free energy flow without any resistance or interference (i.e., lower consciousness or ego).

We have to become the flow itself in order to oscillate it. Opening the higher frequencies requires everything the practitioner has, but still it is not a process of becoming. It cannot be achieved, it can only be realized. In other words, we have to reach the state where the energy flow is self-sustaining and harmonious. By will power alone we cannot sustain it. Also premature stimulation of the energy centers is pointless, if not counterproductive.

At the urge of enlightenment we have to work hard to find the right final tone missing. We have to reach for it and be capable of sustaining it in order to open up the final barrier or resonator. The consciousness shifts smoothly and under control to its natural state (or a physical place where we are able to sense it) where it is out of the way (or in harmony) with the energy flow.

The process is incremental and can take days. The practitioner gets to know the new states and understands their operations. This makes it easier and more familiar along the way. The understanding and comprehension accumulates as well. It is a very natural and harmonious but nevertheless demanding process.

**Some tips for a serious practitioner advanced in the journey:**
- You are not expected to do anything, only realize.
- You cannot force it; it happens when you are totally relaxed and in harmony.
- You must free your body of tension and the urge to achieve.
- You should understand this is a quest of consciousness, not of the body or will power.
- You must realize that until you are love and loving kindness in harmony, you are not there.
- You must follow your instincts and be persistent.
- You should understand it is not a competition or about achievement.
- You should not exhaust yourself; nevertheless, the process is demanding.
- You should be gentle and forgiving; unconditional love is all it takes.
- You know, you can, so you are.

**Advice for beginners:**
- You need firm concentration; once this is sustained, the practitioner is capable of maintaining that concentration even while physically doing something.
- You should understand that meditation only helps you; it is a technique—nothing more.
- You can never be too humble, kind, and loving—these are the real exercise.
- You can progress only through continuous and relentless effort.
- You have to be the harmony and love at all times—so you do not need any particular place or situation to practice it.
- You should realize that frequent meditation sessions are most important, but the real test is your everyday life.
- You need to understand that enlightenment should not be your goal—if it is, consider your motives once again.

# Life and Meditation

Life is eternal harmonious breathing, in and out. Like in breathing, there are three stages to life: in(halation), balance (pauses), and out (exhalation).

Life is oscillation in various energy states. Higher ones contain more intelligence and possibilities than lower ones. Life is an eternal joy of transformation of oscillation levels. These previously mentioned three stages include the harmony within: simply add negative and positive together and these two create a balance, a harmony that can be merged to the oneness or divided once again into three components (1+2). The illusion of isolation and disharmony can be created by observing only from the point of view of either side of the duality. No matter how much relative imbalance either of the sides seems to have, the other counterbalances equal an amount in the opposite direction: the complete duality set is always in balance. These are the unbreakable, eternal, conservation laws of physics.

From a four-dimensional point of view, we can describe reality as an endless, interlinked, and multilayered oscillating vortex. Larger structures include the smaller ones within and the scaling (observation level) is only limited by the observer (which naturally is part of the observation and not outside of it).

What does all this have to do with meditation? We all have our own natural oscillation levels. Meditation is a practice where we try to extend the consciousness or, in other words, increase the oscillation frequency into a permanently higher state. Our personality is the resonator or filter that prevents the energy states going higher permanently. Naturally this is good in a case where one is not tolerant of a high amount of energy and hence could be damaged/destroyed by too much of it. So, meditation is about loosening our seals (or energy filters/dams) and getting ourselves used to higher oscillation frequencies.

Why is meditation so difficult? Imagine that every atom and molecule of your body is oscillating in a certain low frequency. Atoms are moving slowly and it takes a lot of energy to get them excited. While meditating you increase the energy flow within your body and try to make yourself vibrate faster. In the beginning, this is very exhausting and requires a lot of energy—like getting a ship/truck moving from a standstill. It takes less energy to increase the velocity while the movement is already taking place. Similarly, continuous practice of meditation makes reaching the previous oscillation level easier.

Even though the example deals with a "physical" situation, meditation is purely a mental practice. The practitioner needs to focus and align the internal energy flows and use this concentration for expanding the consciousness. The fewer the distractions (thoughts and the like), the more united and efficient the results. Finally, the practitioner is capable of realizing the balance state between/beyond duality and just simply be—become enlightened.

Reaching the harmonious state means that we have permanently (relative term) reached the higher oscillation frequency within the larger context out of which we are a part. The balance state simply means that the practitioner oscillates the frequency of the larger unity without any of his or her own counterwaves or disturbing energies. In other words, the practitioner unites or becomes a drop in the ocean. Naturally, this larger part is increasing its oscillation level as well, but in this context the larger part needs the support of the smaller units to reach its next level. As long as the smaller parts (or critical mass of them) have not increased their individual frequency levels, the larger part cannot increase its incremental level either. For example, think about either the cells within your body or humans in the context of a planet.

Everything is in oscillation. Each and every atom is in its perpetual motion and atoms are never stable and steady, even though our mind persuades otherwise. Each molecule structure or form (larger or smaller) has its own vibration frequency. Remember what an opera singer can do to a wine glass or a synchronously marching division to a bridge? This is exactly what meditation is about. Finding the right tune or note, which you become permanently. Cleansing your thoughts and controlling your emotions are important for the same reason—they are vibrating energy as well. Lower oscillation levels prevent you from progressing. Higher frequencies can be created only by giving them space from the lower ones. And as a reminder, our bodies are 70 percent water, which stores, receives, and transmits vibrations very easily. Conservation and maintaining are always easier than progression.

Just food for thought: What are colors, music, and talk?

# Notes for a Serious Practitioner

Always concentrate on your state of being-ness, never on the mode of being.

Don't try, genuinely be.

Understand you can never be too humble.

Appreciate and be grateful for everything and every single occasion and situation you're facing and living through.

Be patient. Always.

Forgive and be kind to yourself. You can never be too graceful.

Never monitor your progress or try to achieve something— they lead to becoming.

Always acknowledge and be aware of your consciousness. As long as there is something that sees, hears, thinks, feels, or senses, there is still something to learn—the quest is not over.

Do not fixate on anything. There are no excuses. Always be ready to sacrifice everything you have, are, or believe in. Humbleness and honesty with yourself helps.

Always verify your actions and thoughts by your ethical and moral standards. Be honest and watch for half-truths and excuses. Sloppiness is never acceptable.

Only the truth survives.

# Tips for Discovery

Some tips for personal discovery and insight:

1. Focus (quiet your mind).
2. Be persistent.
3. Don't try (don't achieve).
4. Be patient.

# To Change Is Becoming

As long as there is something that changes, the quest is not over. Anything that is not permanent and independent is still becoming; it depends on its external circumstances and, therefore, more or less reacts to these.

A constant state is independent of any outside events or situations as well as any temporal fluctuations such as day or night. How stable is your consciousness?

# Emptiness

*Nothing to declare,*
*nothing to say,*
*nothing to hear,*
*nothing to think;*

*Only silence,*
*accompanying friend,*
*no one to miss,*
*no one to long,*
*lots of actions,*
*many memories,*
*tons of experiences,*
*nothing to look back for;*

*Nothing is the same,*
*everything is the same,*
*they are not relevant;*

*Just being,*
*no expectations,*
*no demands,*
*no claims,*
*no_thing;*

*From here,*
*always here,*
*from one moment,*
*to another,*
*observing,*
*registering,*
*no time,*
*just here,*
*right now;*

*No sadness,*
*no joy,*
*no feelings,*
*no regrets,*
*ready to leave,*
*ready to stay,*
*already being;*

*Calm,*
*relaxed,*
*smooth,*
*peaceful,*
*in harmony;*

*Empty Nest.*

# Short Insights

# Unconditional Love

*It looks at nobody,*
*but sees everyone.*
*Perceives no difference,*
*lays no judgment,*
*still keeps you company.*

*Gives you strength,*
*supports you while you're down,*
*doesn't blame,*
*or put you in to a shame.*

*You are always welcome,*
*never excluded.*
*No matter what happens,*
*or what you do,*
*something is here to stay,*
*and that's for you.*
*Unconditional Love.*

# Beauty

Something fresh.
Anew.
Pure.
Innocent.
Fragile.

Its vulnerability captures its essence. Like a perfect cherry tree blossom in the spring. It radiates its existence without a shadow of doubt. It is now and may not be again. No shame or fear, pure beauty.

# Disappointment

*Disappointment is like happiness,*
*only a bit more serious.*
*It hugs you with its whole reach,*
*and does not let you go.*
*It whispers the story in your ear,*
*the way it should have happened.*
*It grieves and tells you to join,*
*for the mood blue and sad.*

Disappointment is expectations that are let down. It is our "lived" life that did not materialize in the real world. It is real for us and, therefore, it feels concrete. It happens to us like any other real loss that has come our way.

Disappointment can teach us to live in the moment. Why should we be sad for something that has never happened?

# Evolving Path

Life evolves like an ascending spring. Viewed from the side, it reveals its upward spiral while the top view reveals a cyclical continuation. Both ends vanish into the horizon without any end or beginning. They are points that are relative to and only limited by the scale of the observer.

# Fear

Why do we fear everything that is unfamiliar to us (or, to put it differently, why are we uncomfortable with something new?)? Actually, how is it possible to fear something that is not known to us (i.e., understandable, defined, strange)?

We do not. We are only afraid of the things we know and have—we have nothing against the unknown. We simply are afraid of letting go of the past—afraid of the idea that we might have to part from the current state of affairs (i.e., possessions, friends, job, lifestyle, way of living, our point of view, etc.).

How do we stop fearing or getting angry? By letting go. When you give away—there is nothing left. No fear. That's freedom, eternal happiness.

We are not afraid of the fear—only the concept (i.e., idea) of the fear itself.

# Happiness

Unconditional existence without any reciprocity is a true state of happiness. This level of being is not affected by any external circumstances or situations. It is a stable and steady condition, which can be achieved by inner practice and persistence. It is a pure form of being—totally loving and peaceful. Harmony and inner confidence are experienced within and are not, therefore, dependent on the outside world.

Happiness in its purest form is just another expression for sympathy and empathy in their deepest meaning. This means that happiness in its fundamental form is not reflected to the subject itself; it is shared and experienced together with existence and with other beings.

Something that is conditional to circumstances or specific to subjects has nothing to do with happiness. It is a desire or selfish act in disguise. Lasting happiness is omnipotent without an object, a time, or a place. It's eternal and ubiquitous—within our reach at every moment.

# Meaning of Life

(To) Be.

We are just becoming.

As long as we have to become, we are not. When we only are, there is nothing else. A pure state of existence.

# More Precious Than Gold

We are used to valuing almost everything in our lives. Our time and actions as well as the material things surrounding us are measurable. Our days are spent talking, reading, watching, and listening. We communicate and exchange information. Our lives are stuffed with various kinds of data and material. We are hungry for more information and we never seem to get enough. Why?

Because it is easy. We are lazy and do not bother to do anything ourselves. We'd rather recycle and consume something already made. We are even proud of how many details and how much information we can recollect, store, and process. Very nice but unfortunate as well. In other words, we do not create anything new—we recycle.

What is the most scarce and rare resource around us? Actually it is so common that if we used it even in tiny fractions of its entire potential, things would not be the same again. Sadly, this seems to be so hard that barely anyone has the guts to practice it on a continual basis.

Just think.

# Physical Existence

Physical existence is
a mask,
disguise,
larva of a butterfly,
working cloth,
marionette,
platform,
embodiment,
avatar,
outer jacket,
transformer,
agent,
shelter,
a shell that hides the pearl.
Our physical existence is a reflection of the essence. The reminder of the real—a replication of the current state. A mirror for the beholder.

# Recycling

Most of us are like TV sets. We receive information and reproduce it as it has been sent to us. Often, we just store things to our memory and retract them when they are needed. The reproduction, from the content perspective, is more or less the same, but the quality may have been lowered in the process.

Watching and criticizing movies is easy. Coming up with a creative script and vision is another case entirely. The same applies to our thinking as well. We read and absorb vast amounts of data that we do not analyze. Most of our so-called education is based on recycling of information. One is taught to find, memorize, and rephrase information. Individual thinking and consideration are not highly appreciated or encouraged. Still, everyone has the capabilities of developing his or her own thinking.

Creative functions require concentration, will, and vision. First one needs to be able to formulate a vision or goal and then be able to materialize it into a physical form. Thinking is like making a movie. It all starts from will and desire to express yourself (e.g., a great storyline). This then has to be formulated somehow into a structure that consists of the logic and systematic setting (a script). Finally, one needs to be able to realize the concept into a production where the final product is a visible movie. All these stages take energy and persistence: one gets better with practice.

Thinking is considered to be hard and nonnatural for humans; therefore, it is a scarce resource. We are too lazy to use our brain. It requires effort. Nevertheless, we appreciate writers, composers, directors, painters, scientists, and all those great minds who are able to create something beautiful and innovative. All of us have different skills and talents. Creative thinking can lead us to amazing discoveries. How about trying? You may be surprised of the results: *Cogito ergo sum.*

# Time Excuse

Our greatest excuse is time. Either we do not have enough of it or we have too much of it. Still, we can only live now, forever. Future is only an illusion we project based on our experiences and understanding. Past is a regenerated memory and experience collection we re-produce according to our current understanding and point of view. All this can only happen right now. And still they are all only pure image forms—nothing else.

We continuously fool ourselves. We play this game by saying to ourselves that we will do this or that and gain or progress in a specific manner in the future. But all this is done in a way that implicitly says we are currently lacking something and will do the hard part later. Time is our excuse: "I need time to develop/study and so on." This would be fine if we really would deliver on what we promised. Unfortunately, we often change our mind along the process. It is more important (i.e., easier) to be in the constant mode of changing than actually achieving or being.

We escape the current moment almost all the time. We are not happy about how we are at the moment and, therefore, we like to comfort ourselves by saying that this is not the real me but wait an X amount of time, and I will be this. This game is endless. Either we crave the past or envision an imaginary dream world of the future.

When do we have time to actually be? Being requires that we also see and hear in the moment. It requires unbiased, objective observation and facing reality as it is, right now. No bias toward the past or the future—only the bare truth. Have you ever realized who you really are or appear to be?

# Trust

Trust is about relying on someone, letting ourselves be vulnerable and fragile, totally dependent on someone. It is a token of something pure and innocent, a way of expressing confidence and pure beliefs. Something beautiful and overwhelming. Appreciation without apprehension. A bond that if you are careful will last through almost anything, but with a misstep can be broken as easily as any china.

Its strength is in its vulnerability. Its kindness and willingness to sacrifice and be naked in front of the other grasp its essence. Trust is something you cannot fake. Either you have it or you do not have it. It can be built upon but once lost it is almost impossible to repair. It is a fine line that is so easy to cross and so hard to be noticed. Trust is like love. It's up to us to make the choice. By choosing to trust, you never lose. It is not about the outcome but the intent. Nobody ever wins anything if there is nothing to be trusted. Someone has to start—why not let it be you? It is all about trust, and the final outcome is not up to you.

# Wanting

When you want something you also state that you don't have something. Your object of wanting is the very thing you're missing. In other words, you're declaring your imperfectness. There is something in you that still requires and is in need.

The person who is at peace and has achieved a state of calmness needs no thing. He or she has everything. What was it that you needed?

# Zen Thoughts

*How does it feel to dive with a diving suit? How about being a water molecule?*

*What's reality like from eternity's point of view?*

*Who talks by silence, does the most.*

*We think we are. Where am I while sound asleep?*

*We are only our thoughts, but who thinks us?*

*I am either sound asleep (i.e., unconscious), dreaming, or awake. When am I?*

*How can we see something we know nothing about?*

*One thinks but never knows.*

# Reality and Ego

# Presence

*All there is,*
*is right here and just now;*
*Don't wait,*
*don't travel,*
*shift forward or delay;*
*Postpone to escape,*
*move to forget;*
*Still it does not matter—*
*all there is,*
*is right here and just now.*

*Pre-set for presence,*
*and set free,*
*or reset.*
*To be and not to be—together,*
*is the key.*
*Live real and*
*realize,*
*right here and just now.*

*Cannot force,*
*cannot push,*
*no way to rush;*
*Distant yourself,*
*just now and right here,*

*for two beings,*
*aligned into one;*
*Living together,*
*peacefully and in harmony,*
*without fights,*
*of dominance.*

*Presence is intense,*
*only in one,*
*with full knowledge,*
*and understanding,*
*of right here and just now;*
*To be—always,*
*and even without,*
*a physical presence,*
*makes sense,*
*only,*
*right here and just now.*

# Reality

Reality is a subjective phenomenon. It consists of our personal understanding of the structures around us. It is an interpretation based on inner perception and insights. Our reality is something that we take as the ultimate truth for us, something that we cannot question and that is the basis for our existence. It is the building block and foundation upon which everything else is placed.

Subjective reality has nothing to do with the physical world around us. Our reality is just based on the observations and conclusions we have drawn and understood with the best of our perception. One way to illustrate this is to look back in history. Not so many centuries ago people believed that the world was flat. It was a nonquestionable fact, like the presence of day and night or the soil underneath us. What happened later on was that humankind made more precise observations of the physical world and was able to adjust its understanding and perceptions based on new evidence. Today, no one can seriously claim that the world is a flat surface. We can take a flight and observe it with our very eyes. Our subjective reality is dependent on our capabilities and, therefore, it is unique to everyone. Also, it evolves over time but the physical reality remains the same.

We are children in a larger scale; when we grow up, our perception and behavior change accordingly. Grown-ups do less kids' stuff and their understanding of the issues are altered together with experience and better understanding. Humankind goes through the same process, but the cycle is naturally longer. Humankind's progress takes generations, whereas children expand their consciousness each year. History demonstrates this development. The United Nations Universal Declaration of Human Rights was declared for all people on earth just under sixty years ago. Physical wars and abuse of power are less tolerated now than in the beginning of the twentieth century. The progress has its unit in generations—not in years. All it takes is our internal reality to develop. Each individual contributes to the process, and collectively we declare who we are and what our perception of the reality is—our truth.

# Division

Everything we see, have, are, and live within is based on two structures: the substance (i.e., the essence) and its representation (manifestation). The appearance is the structure that is easy to comprehend and is the only truth existing for the inexperienced.

Only the wise can separate the representation from the substance. The ignorant regards the appearance as the essence and creates more confusion around. Everything has this twofold existence and, therefore, any act or deed can either be banal or of essence. It cannot be acknowledged only from the representation. The paradox is that being able to reproduce the appearance has nothing to do with the substance—nor does it have to do with the comprehension. It is easier to reproduce and arrange the representation than to realize the substance underneath. However, nothing has any real value and meaning without the substance.

The substance never has a physical appearance. It can only be associated with something tangible, but it cannot be captured by it. For example, what is a wedding ring without love?

# Our Quest

Plato's ideal world consists of perfect items. Those items are not present in our visible world, still we can get a feeling of these perfect items by the world around us. We are living around those items—only the proportion of the perfectness varies. We recognize these forms, and we desire for more. We would like them to stay with us, forever. Our endless quest is to reach for these ideal items and surround ourselves by them. Our life is a quest for ideal forms that cannot stay in a material format but can reflect parts of life's perfect existence, for example, a quest for the Holy Grail, which is not a material kind of quest. Therefore, the material sought is eternal—ideas can only be found in their original form.

Some people remind us about humbleness, beauty, passion, sympathy, love, intelligence, humor, selflessness, and so on. These ideas are reflected in the person. We feel that these items are something noble and very familiar to us. We are naturally attracted to and moved by these ideas. Similarly, we can find the same forms and ideas in the world around us. The nature is always beautiful, and our humanmade art captures the essence of many timeless shapes of ideas. Still, like Plato said, we cannot capture the formless into a physical shape entirely. Only parts of it can be present, at best.

Next time you meet a person or see an object that captures some fraction of the ideal form, ask yourself this question: Are you attracted to the person/object or to the form it represents? This is something worth considering for a while. If it is really the person or item, then it should not matter if it is changing over time—maybe reflecting less or decaying the ideal form that caught your attention in the first place. Our disappointments in life reflect the fact that we fall in love with the idea and not the object it represents. When the object itself changes we are taken by surprise and long for the idea it used to resonate.

Ideas and forms are eternal. They are always present but they cannot be captured in time and space. They can be experienced only as they come and when they come—in that very moment—the rest is pure illusion and shadows.

# Our World

The world we know exists only in our mind. It is real for us, but it is not to be found elsewhere. We are dependent on our sensations coming from our five main doors (i.e., sight, hearing, smell, taste, touch). The world for us is constructed ultimately in our mind. For example, colors do not exist in the physical world. All objects are colorless. Similarly, our eyes work like lenses in a camera. They get a mere two-dimensional picture as any other lens. It is our mind that puts all this together and creates the world for us. This abstraction is a three-dimensional spatial world where time is applied as well. It is an illusion, like matter. There is no such thing as matter. Studying a bit of physics, from Newton's revelations to Einstein and quantum mechanics, verifies these points.

In short, the great *maya*, illusion, is that the world we know is only a thought, an idea—it is a picture with many objects but, nevertheless, a picture—nothing more, nothing less. No matter what you do, it is all within your mind—even when external to your body, it's still within your mind.

How do you know that you are dreaming while asleep? You don't. It is as real as anything for you—once again a mere thought or an idea but sound proof that our mind is capable of constructing a three-dimensional world even without external sensations. Nevertheless pure pictures that are real for us.

How can you wake up from the illusion while awake? You cannot. No matter what you do, even when you realize the truth, your mind still determines to draw the illusion for you. It just does not have the same impact anymore. Living in a world of ideas or created objects (i.e., pictures, thoughts) does not put us in direct touch with the real existence. We are tied to our sensations. Those are our only link to the existence.

Our mind constructs a derivative for us—its interpretation of the sensations, which we then perceive and become aware of. We only know these perceptions—nothing about the real existence.

# The Real Reality

For us the visible reality is the real thing. We associate ourselves with it and respond to it as well. Often, we feel uncomfortable and find hard to match with the world around us. Inside we are distressed with the outer reality. It does not reflect our ideal inner state.

Throughout the ages it has been said that the visible world is not real or it is called as an illusion or *maya*. Plato, in his famous *The Allegory of the Cave*, described the same dark cave and shadows that the people we're obliged to observe—not the true figures or the outside world. In the modern world, these metaphors are hard to grasp and to realize.

Still, nothing could be more true. Maybe the phrasing could be different, but the original message remains intact—always. This visible reality is the one where we communicate and observe. Yet we are present in other planes as well. They are not visible to us, but we are members on those ones as well. Beside the physical body we also have our feelings and emotions as well as our mental capabilities. They are as real for anyone as the physical world itself, even though we cannot see them.

So, where's the real reality and what does it mean? The world every wisdom tries to illustrate and refer to is the reality of thoughts. That is where anything is first created—it is thought out. Only after that can it be expressed and materialized. No matter whether we are talking about going shopping, building a house, or even speaking. First it has to be created and then it is a matter of realization, depending on the case at hand.

A thought without any feeling is not complete. Saying "I love you" without a feeling is meaningless. Similarly, the feeling or the passion/desire has to be combined with the thought. Together they are something. This applies to talking, building a house, or any other matter. (The third required element is power or will to execute or carry out the matter, but this is just a hint for the considerate reader and not relevant to the topic.)

Why should we not focus on the outside world and instead purely concentrate on the inner higher reality? No matter where you look, you find the wise words that encourage us to look inside or, as Pythagoras has so nicely put it: "Man know thyself then thou shalt know the Universe and God." These should not be understood in a manner that one ignores the visible world or isolates himself or herself from the world. The purpose is to encourage us to focus on the essence or the source where everything is really taking place and where we can have control and real influence on the visible world.

First this may sound quite bizarre or contrary, but just consider how much in control of your world you really are. Are you pretending to be in control or just really facing the facts that you are only an observer for the occurring events? A feeling of being in control is not the same as having a real influence on the issues and understanding what is really causing them. Can you have a peaceful and happy life?

Some people can. And they have followed Pythagoras' advice. They have realized that in order to achieve something, we have to look inside and find it first there and only after that can it materialize in the outer world. Actually, nothing can prevent it from occurring should the desire be strong and persistent enough. Why is this so hard to believe and start to implement?

Simply because we are used to living and looking outside of ourselves. We take it for granted that by doing something in the outside world we can make something happen in our desired manner. But what happens when you start to do this? You create a perpetuity machine without even realizing it or having a chance to jump out. Often, only the final desperation makes the person get out of the cul-de-sac and start to look inside himself or herself for strength. Only then can something start to happen. The reason for this is very simple. The outside reality is just a mere cause of the activities that happened before—that is, the results or the reflections of the mental thoughts and feelings. *Nothing can ever change in the outer reality until the thought and emotional structures are changed accordingly.*

We have to first "see" and "feel or believe" (together) the desired outcome and only then can it start to happen. If you just look at the current state of the visible world and take it for granted without any creative and passionate effort, then nothing will ever improve or change; actually, the opposite often happens. A negative spiral is created—things look so bad and hence I will be so depressed and so on. Naturally a positive inspiration and feeling is also possible—then only the sky is the limit, isn't it?

Why is this so hard to believe, still? Because we do not see the real reality and thus we do not consider it matters. We think that we can think, feel, or say whatever we feel like without much consideration or significance. And look the state of the world today! Have we been able to live in peace and love each other as humans? How about your thoughts and feelings—are they only loving and peaceful every day and toward everything, permanently?

Maybe we should start to consider more carefully the wise words repeated so often to us throughout the centuries. We have people among us who have achieved a permanent state of tranquility and happiness. Even the latest science does not disprove this. Einstein and quantum mechanics can do wonders if you want to study them. Why is it that the observer affects the observation or, to put it differently, why does the thought affect the thinker?

# Reflector

Our world consists of atoms and smaller particles, quarks. The scale does not end here, but all the same, everything is still energy. Therefore, one can say that we are focused energy states. Our physical bodies are built on atoms (and other smaller particles) that are held together by internal forces physics is still discovering. Our existence is based on dynamic and continuous flow of energy that is focused and organized in a manner that keeps our structure "stable" over time. Otherwise, our physical form would not exist from one moment to another and we would be dissolved around the place.

From one point of view, we are a pure energy structure or concentration. Everything that happens to us is energy as well, for example, the sights we see, the sounds we hear, the sensations we get from hot or cold, pressure, and so on. In other words, we are a reflector of different energies, no more and no less, like a mirror that reflects the light directed to it. In our case, we can also be an active party—not just a microphone reflecting sound energy (waves) coming its way. Using the same metaphor, we can also be a loudspeaker and amplifier, depending on the case. Altogether our existence consists of energy flows and states that are enclosing and surrounding us.

Our senses are adapted to a certain very limited range of energy levels. For example, our visual sight is based on receiving light spectrum from violet (400nm) to red (700nm). This scale includes the colors of the rainbow. In other words, a certain very narrow range of light frequencies comprises our visible world or our seeable reality. Outside of our senses lie most of the electromagnetic spectrum including gamma and X-rays, ultraviolet and infrared rays, and radar, to name a few. These wavelengths are visible to us only by special arrangements. Still they exist and constitute the world around us in addition to the visible light range. So, how was it: "Seeing is believing" or "receiving is realizing."

We as reflectors are capable of receiving a certain type of energy flow. Our subjective reality is dependent on the senses we have and their capabilities. How different would our life be if we had some other spectra to reflect as well? After all, a reflector is capable of vibrating only in the scale it has been tuned for. Most of the vibes are beyond our belief and understanding—as of today, at least.

# Relative

Our existence is relative. We are only in relation to some-thing. Nothing has any meaning or significance per se, unless it is in relation to something. The world outside of us just is. We give it the meaning and the purpose, and it has the signif-icance and relevance we define and understand it to have. Because our existence is evolving in the now time, this also means that we create the world again and again over time. Our perceptions and understanding change and, therefore, the surroundings and the world have different meaning and relevance for us at different moments.

Relativeness enables us to experience and learn more about ourselves. It gives us the opportunity to compare and value things. We give the world the meaning and, therefore, it also reflects our perception and understanding. We live and expe-rience life in relation to our own consciousness; it provides us the measurement and the yardstick. To simplify this concept, we would say we are the world and the world is us. Nothing happens outside of ourselves—everything in the world has to do with us. Our existence is based purely on gaining under-standing and realization about ourself. Self-realization is only possible when we put things into a relationship, and we can-not realize ourself if there is nothing to compare to or distin-guish from. Our individualism and separation ceases the moment we do not need the concept of relativeness anymore. Until then, everything is relative—and subjective.

# Something Eligible

Everything with a form and shape falls into the trinity of creation, sustenance, and dissolution. These three states are inevitable and they materialize in time space. Each manifestation is a child of its age; it uses the concepts, structures, and ways of the current relative reality. It has a limited existence and relevance as well. Nothing lasts forever in time-space.

It is a poor representation and characterization when something that has no shape or form has to be presented in static and descriptive terms that automatically limit its dynamic nature (i.e., real essence) to abstraction. This relative manifestation is bound to its surroundings and can be interpreted only in its original environment and nature (also in time).

This means that any attempt that tries to capture something beyond time-space limitations is doomed to fail. At best, we are capable of providing approximations that observe only a part of the concept in question—never the entire concept itself.

A metaphor to illustrate the point: filming a live event can only capture a part of the real action, not the smell, atmosphere, and other parts of the live event itself that took place. More importantly, filming cannot reproduce the actual activity—it can only describe and capture a limited part of it (i.e., some of the visual aspects).

The relevance is that we stick to these representations and give them meanings they originally never had. They start to live a life of their own. They do not compare with the actual essence they were used to represent. A replica never becomes better; it does not exceed the original.

How about we stop chasing the shadows and focus on the source instead?

# Doing without the Doer

Why is the doer so important? Or, to be more specific, when is the doer important? In most of the cases, the performer is relevant only when we are doing it ourselves. We emphasize the subject more than the actual deed or the doing process. In brief, when we are the subjects it is very important but when others are the contributors, we are not as interested. Confusing?

This is very evident if we observe our own life. Just think back to the last movie or theatre play you saw or book you read. Who were the actors and authors? Do you remember? Some of us have naturally better name-recall memory, but still. We concentrate and focus on the substance itself and not so much on the individual actors' contributions and relevance per se. A theatre play is a team effort for the overall atmosphere and experience combined from individual contributions. Similarly, the author creates the novel but for us the storyline and the substance is the thing. When we are the doer, it is something exceptional and unique but when others do it, that's a different case—it is something usual or rather normal at least. The same applies when we are simply talking. It is a rare skill to be a good listener because we often prefer talking to listening. Listening is often the opportunity to think what we are going to say next, isn't it?

So why is it so important who is doing the action? In reality, it is not relevant at all. The most important thing is the deed itself and its effects. The only one who craves recognition is our own mind. Our mind lives from our attention and focus. It needs our undivided notice and recognition of importance. There are many words for this type of behavior: greed, selfishness, vanity, ego, and so on. The doer is important only in conditional and relative terms. If the actions were totally selfless, the performer would be irrelevant. In all the other cases there is some conditional reason or purpose for the deed as a vehicle to something else. It does not serve a purpose itself.

The world does not need the doers—only the actions. Therefore, the doer is not relevant—actually it is only an illusion. This imaginary performer is living only in our own mind. We would still exist without it and perform the same tasks and duties. The only thing missing from the picture would be the self-appraisal and egocentric behavior. Who needs them, anyone?

# I—Who?

When you are angry ask yourself: Who is angry?

When you are disappointed ask yourself: Who is disappointed?

When you are in need of something ask yourself: Who needs?

When you are sad ask yourself: Who is sad?

Why is it that it is always the external world that is to be blamed? And yet, all of your answers start with I (with a capital letter). Who is this I (who is angry, disappointed, in need, and sad)?

This mysterious I interacts with the world but still takes no responsibility for his or her actions. Why does this I always projects the reasons for hardship and excuses on the external world? Interaction requires at least two parties.

How about sorting out things with this I first and dealing with the world later?

# Me, Myself, and I

Limited understanding leads to misinterpretations and imperfect actions. These actions are perceived emotionally and assumed to be conducted with full intention and understanding of the causes and consequences by the actor. This realization raises strong emotional sensations in the receiver and causes responses that are not based on full consideration (i.e., something one is regretting later on as too excessive and out of line). Responses and consequences are something that are not intended by the initial actor but simply caused by the limited capabilities of perception and understanding by both parties. From here, things just get worse and, after a while, neither party has any control of the matter and the original starting point has lost any significance and relevance. This is how a vicious circle is created and the results are observable around the world every day. And everything starts just from our limited capabilities to perceive and understand the world we're living in.

Our own standing point is very important to us. We regard it as the right one because it is so real to us—we have no doubts. Therefore, it is the "truth" and because it is so obvious, there cannot be any possibilities of misunderstandings by other people; they simply cannot ignore it and be so blind as not to see simple "facts" that even we can understand. But they do not act accordingly, and their behavior is so much beyond our belief that we cannot stand it. It's too much, and we need to do something about it…

Yet everybody lives in his or her own subjective reality. We are fixed to our own needs and requirements. Our thinking is full of "us." We get offended, we have the most at stake, we have to give up, we have to sacrifice, we are not benefiting, and so on. It is that We that prevents us from making a difference. As long as it is our needs that have to be appreciated and fulfilled first, nothing will ever change. Everybody clings to his or her own mind-set and perception of the world. And we have an urge to be right—and let others to know it as well.

One needs to learn to give away. Over time, we acknowledge seeing a broader picture where different opinions and points of view can be presented and maintained without a need to conflict. There is no need to be right or gain something. The whole notion of "us" is just something of our own fabrication. We only need to let it go—and that's the only thing we are giving away, in reality.

# Process Point of View

Process is something that is not permanent and it serves a specific purpose. It is not the end means but just a way to carry out something.

We could be seen as a set of processes. Our physical body changes over time. It creates new cells and destroys the old ones. It is in a continuous process of keeping itself alive—a biological process. More interestingly, our consciousness could be seen as processes as well. Our mind consists of various processes that come and go. Our state of mind is not permanent. It changes all the time. Our moods, feelings, thoughts, and observations keep us busy. These sensations always appear from somewhere, stay for a while, and then disappear. We cannot freeze them or make them stay. Also, our self-image is not permanent. All the time we re-create the concept of ourselves by defining in the now time our past (i.e., memories) and the projected future constituting our current perception and definition of who we are.

After breaking apart in very broad sense our existence into various sets of processes, it is a fair question to ask where we are. Who are we—are we just the total sum of the processes happening in us? Where is the self?

How about if there is no self, only processes that keep going for a certain period of time? Processes do not need self. They just carry on going. They flow in and out. The combination of these processes creates the concept of self. Our mind is the perception of these temporary processes that gives it a point of view and illusion of "being." It exists as long as there are enough processes in motion. Still, it does not control the actions. It cannot create the process or reproduce them. It can only adapt and accept—and realize its own place in the puzzle. And by doing so it disappears as artificial. But the processes continue flowing in and out until their time has come.

# Stop Worrying

Many times it looks like we live for our worries. They surround us and follow us everywhere we go. There might be a lot to worry about or just many tiny issues that pile up and make us uncomfortable. Worries are always subjective and they also evolve over time. We learn to cope in life and do not stress about the same things over and over again. Our subjects of worrying change, but the basic concept remains intact—we keep constantly stressing about our future and survival.

We build up expectations and then start to stress about possible future outcomes. What-if scenarios with different variations fill our mind and we cannot get past the mind's loops. Some of these worries may turn into obsessions and even disturb our sleep and daily activities.

We worry because we cannot imagine anything else that we are aware of. This means that our limited perception and knowledge does not allow us to solve the puzzles our mind has put in front of us to solve. Often, we are going around with our thoughts that are dependent on factors that are beyond our control. We desperately would like to know what happens before the actual reality materializes. We cannot stand uncertainty. Actually, we are only afraid of the uncertainty. Even knowing what is going to happen, no matter how bad, is more bearable than the great uncertainty.

We can continue worrying about everything in our life nonstop. We can never know the future and, therefore, there are always possibilities to come up with new unknown issues or situations. This is not necessary, however. We do not need to stress about life—it's totally unnecessary. The paradox just is that we have to realize this first and then we are liberated from the catch-22. It is the same with most of the important facts of life—we have to live them true, gain an insight first.

We have to see the pattern that our mind repeats every time. It identifies some unknown issues and starts to process them. This way, our mind keeps us busy—after all, our mind exists only when we think.

The process to stop worrying can be started by gradual steps: accomplish the small things first and move to bigger and more significant items later. When we start to realize that things do get sorted out and worrying really is unnecessary, we will finally stop worrying altogether. Worrying has a lot to do with self-confidence and acceptance. We have to know and trust ourselves. When we are confident that we can handle and manage in life no matter what comes our way, this inner confidence will guide us and provide us with inner peace. We stop worrying about other people and their responses and thoughts about us. Our greatest concern will then be to act according to our own intuitions and feeling about what are the right choices and actions in the situations at hand. As well, we realize that things that are beyond our control should not be worried about at all—we simply have to accept them, as they are and without any denial or resistance. Facing the facts is often the most difficult part. We do not want to admit the reality, even though we might somehow realize it. It is just something too painful to accept.

By worrying we lose a lot of energy. Our mind keeps us occupied and in the negative thoughts that tie us in a destructive loop. Instead of finding solutions or positive outcomes, we are trapped in a loop of thoughts that lead nowhere. The time we use wondering about our possible future we cannot then use to find and identify new opportunities that may bypass us in the meanwhile. Often, the very answers we look for are offered to us but we simply cannot see them—we are fixed in our thinking patterns and projected outcomes. In other words, we are too busy worrying and life, and many good moments and opportunities as well, passes us by.

Those people with great wisdom have always said that we should stop worrying. Still, we do not believe them. Our life has taught us that it will give us unpleasant surprises and living hurts. We are afraid of the outcomes. Therefore, we constantly try to avoid any imaginable disturbance or negative incident. Still, these incidents come when we least expect them—we cannot avoid them. We even die one day—no matter how much we worry or think about it. Worrying does not help us to live. Actually, it does not allow us to experience and enjoy life as it comes, and it keeps us obsessed about some future incident that potentially can happen or may not happen at all. The only one who loses in this game is us. Worrying is time wasted without any positive outcomes expected—one of the great lessons to learn in life.

# Who Am I?

Have you ever considered the question where are you really?

Let's start by defining a house: What is a house? Usually it is built for a purpose—it has some relevance and function. A house is built up from various different components that are combined and put together from basic materials and minerals. In other words, a combination of materials put together in a certain order is called a house. This house is not outside of the world from which it is put together. A house can be old, young, stylish, ugly, ruined, or abandoned. At the end of its existence, it is again just various materials in another order that is no longer called a house. So what was the house?

OK, back to us. Who am I? Am I the body that is combined in a particular order from stem cells? Now we have learned to replace our broken arms, hearts, and other organs with new ones. We can even start to grow entirely new body parts from our very own stem cells. We can be young, old, beautiful, ugly, sick, or healthy. And at the end of the day we are just a bunch of materials in different order and we are called dead. So what was me?

As we defined, a house is a combination of things from its surroundings. It is not outside of the world. It is part of the world. But still the house is something that is separate because we call it a house. If it were not separate, why should it have a name? Something nonexistent cannot be seen or realized. A separation means that it has boundaries and can be put in relation to something.

When we are very young we do not know the difference between our own body and the outside world. We learn this separation from others. We can observe and sense things around us that are not us. We do not feel them or cannot control them. So we come to a conclusion that they must not be us. Similarly, in the way we call a bunch of materials laid together in a particular order a house, other people call us by name. Other people define us and we learn to be that *whaterthename* they have given us.

House has a particular function or purpose. But what is our purpose? Why are we at the same time separate from the world but still part of the world as well (we do not live outside of the world)? We are a bunch of materials put together in a particular order and we have a certain concentration of atoms or energy from which other people recognize us. So could this separation serve a purpose? Why should we be separated from the world if that would not be meaningful? No one would build a house if the house would not have any function. There would not even be a word *house* in that case. A separation named house within the world serves a purpose for us—it shelters and gives us a place to stay. But a house cannot acknowledge itself. We can. Why should we be aware of our separation and existence if that would not serve a purpose? It would be totally strange to use energy to put something together without any purpose.

So, who am I? For sure I am this separation called by my name. I should be also part of the world because I'm built upon the materials found in the world. But when my heart is replaced or my leg is lost I do not vanish with them. So they are not me. There seems to be other people like me. They behave the same, they talk and communicate. Their existence seems similar to mine. Still, they seem not to be me. There are also other living things that are called animals and plants. I'm not so sure of them because they do not communicate like humans do. But I'm sure they exist as well. They live outside of me.

Somehow it is difficult to go further from here. There really does not seem to be a me, only this separation within the world that is recognized by others. They have defined me, and I am built upon things found in the world. My conclusion is that there is no me or I could say as well that I am the world because I'm part of it and live in it. This temporary separation called me is like a house. But what is a house? My purpose is to realize the separation as an illusion and as not more than atoms laid in a particular order. A temporary concept built upon to realize the concept of me—and its oneness with the world. A separation to realize its oneness. And then shall I be no more separated.

# Ready

*We are free,*
*to stay,*
*or to go;*
*No one holds,*
*but us.*

*We have so much,*
*to do,*
*and are so busy to achieve.*
*We hold tight,*
*for all we know.*

*It's up to us,*
*when everything is done,*
*and there is nothing,*
*more to do,*
*cling,*
*or achieve.*

*We just get enough,*
*realize,*
*and undo.*
*Nothing to learn,*
*no more to gain,*
*nothing to achieve,*
*nothing to lose,*
*only no thing.*

*We give up,*
*let go,*
*prepare,*
*for the unknown.*

# Separation

# Why

*Why are we sad?*
  *Because we are not happy.*

*Why are we excited?*
  *Because we are not bored.*

*Why are we in love?*
  *Because we are not lonely.*

*Why are we upset?*
  *Because we are not content.*

*When we realize,*
  *Then we only are.*

# Dualism

We need dualism to live and experience. The list of examples is basically infinite: day and night, good and bad, dark and light, male and female, healthy and sick, and so on. Without the opposite concept, we would not recognize the difference; all would be the same. And when there is nothing else, we cannot imagine or appreciate anything else—it would not exist for us. This would make learning difficult because there would be no way to compare things and occasions. How could we appreciate life if there was no death?

Still, we are blind. We do not want to see that one cannot get the other without expecting the other to occur as well. We're after happiness but we're afraid of sorrow. We're after wealth but cannot stand poorness. We get disappointed when the other event appears. Usually it's a great disaster or bad karma/luck. And when the positive occurrence meets us, we have deserved it—naturally. It's quite funny, I must say. Unfortunately, this is how we live and act. The consequences of our blindness are not nice to see. As much happiness as we create, we create at least the same amount of sorrow by not seeing the full picture. Our selfish behavior creates a mess that others have to solve.

Most of the dualisms are our own creation. They do not actually exist in our physical world. Think, for example, of good and bad or beauty and ugliness. Each person formulates his or her own perception of these concepts. Things are just what they are—we create the meaning, the dualism. If we would see the pure, true existence, there would be far fewer surprises and disappointments and far fewer ideological wars or "acts of rightness." But are we able to learn to live without the dualistic existence reminding us the lesson every day? For instance, humankind has not learned to live in peace since the first day of our existence—the concept seems so difficult to master. Yet if you hit someone with a hammer and the other person gets hurt, he or she might just hit back. Then you are hurt as well, and everybody is worse off. Get the full picture?

# Give Away

We are captured in duality. Space and time are our destiny. As long as we are learning this lesson, we are under the role of dualism. Life and death, day and night, good and bad. Action and reaction. Everything we do or think causes a reaction—and the action has its consequences.

As long as we have meanings and bonds to this dualistic world, we are going to go through the lessons. But gradually, very slowly, we are starting to give away. Let it go. We are no longer carried away by either the positive or the negative aspect. Nor are we trying to seek the one and avoid the other. Actually, the whole occurrence becomes irrelevant. It is the same no matter which way it turns. We grow to acknowledge and ignore. No great feelings or attachments—just a pure flow of actions and reactions. Step by step, a bigger part of our life becomes about giving away—letting it go. And finally we are free. We have totally given away the duality, and the previous polarization turns into unity. We have learned the lesson—to give away.

# Longing

We live in a state of constant longing. The current moment seems never to be enough. When we've reached one thing, we immediately long for something else. The grass is always greener on the other side. The main idea here is that we are wanting: always and for something. But what are we longing for?

Our yearning is a sensation we have a hard time describing. It is something that surrounds us but still we are not able to explain it exactly. Longing is something formless that encircles us. It is a notion in us that seeks existence and expression through us. One could say that longing uses us as its vehicle for material existence.

In practice, this means that we project our yearning for a physical or tangible form. We attach our desires for some objects or objectives. Depending on the circumstances, it can be a person we are missing, a better job, our own apartment, our spouse, wealth, or an occupation, to name a few. No matter the subject, the important point is that for us, it is something concrete. We have a hard time separating the object from the subject. We mark the object of the longing and start to regard it as the means of improving our state of being (i.e., our inner condition).

We are all familiar with the results. The instant we have achieved that something that we wanted, we are after something else. We are not satisfied, which was the whole purpose of the issue. Now we are after something else. So, what actually happens?

Longing makes us active. It drives us to experience and face different challenges in life. What would happen if we would not long for anything? Nothing. But there would not be much progress either. If no one is either after or lacking anything, because longing implies a condition where the subject is incomplete and seeks the missing component, nothing would improve or change.

It is important to identify this continuous process we are going through. One should realize that longing is not "us"—we can never become fulfilled by any means outside of our inner being. Therefore, if we can see through this longing and ignore its quest, we are already closer to being "complete." We are not running around and reaching for something illusionary. All we need to do is to identify our behavioral patterns and make conscious actions instead of commit blind obedience. How about reaching for nonlonging?

# The Other

How can we learn about ourselves? By facing the Other.

Some time ago, I wrote about relationships and referred to Martin Buber. Emmanuel Levinas was inspired by the work of Buber and became one of the greatest French philosophers of the twentieth century. Levinas pointed out that we can only learn about ourselves by facing other beings that are not us (the Other). We cannot share our existence—we can only talk about it. And it is the human interaction that makes the learning possible. We have to meet the Other, face to face.

In *Humanism of the Other*, Levinas raised ethics to a higher level than just a discussion of pure ontology and knowledge about being.

*Totality and Infinity* describes the difference between the infinity and the self. It explains how we can be the self, the subject, that seems to be separated from the infinity. Levinas clarified the reason for the subjectivity and the illusion of separation from the Other and the infinity.

The purpose of subjectivity is to teach us about the unity but one can learn about it only by being separated and being in relation to other beings. And this lesson seems to be so hard for us. We regard ourselves as special and unique. We are not like the others. But the bottom line is that we are all the same—part of the infinity and the unity. Our perceived separation is an illusion that temporarily hides us from the truth. And this lesson seems to take ages for us. Individualism and selfishness are the popular themes of our time. Still, deep inside we feel and know that all life is equal—part of the same, the one.

# Ownership

Owning means that the owner of something has the right to exclude others from using it and has a title to control the subject. How much can we really own and is ownership freedom?

Some time ago, I wrote about the concept of ownership. Because of the current discussion in politics, it's interesting to consider the other aspects of ownership—the sense of control and freedom.

Usually people want to own things in order to secure something. They feel more secure when they own the house rather than rent it. When you own something, you have something "real." Ownership is just a word like any other. Nothing else. We could define it as well to mean a monopoly or right of exclusion.

By calling owning a right of exclusion, we might realize more of its nature. By owning, we exclude. We get something and deny others access to something. Amusingly enough, this is in many cases the physical reality as well. Wealthy nations have tight border controls and rich people fence themselves into their properties.

Currently, only a few people in the developed world possess most of the resources and wealth in the world. This exclusion creates disharmony and restlessness. This is not just the case between wealthy U.S. and Europe versus third world countries, but also within nations. The United States could be a case in point, but one could consider many other nations as well. The bigger the contrast, the larger the resources required to keep the situation in control. Security and military budgets are growing every year and terrorist attacks are becoming part of everyday life. Is it true that the more we own the more freedom we create?

It seems to be the opposite. The more we own, the more we have to worry about. If our personal sense of control and security is tied to the concept of owning, then the more we own the more we have to lose. Our possessions become part of our existence. They are part of our ego and ourself. Any threat to our possessions not only means living without something but also poses a direct threat to our own existence (i.e., our sense of security and control; freedom). What might have started as a pure means of getting a title to something easily turns into a vehicle for gaining personal security and a sense of freedom. And it's no wonder that at this stage, things get complicated. And usually nasty as well. Now it's personal. My possessions are part of my existence; they define who I am. The more the better—without them I am nothing. Very physical and very real. Very personal.

Seldom can we share the wealth with others and keep the ownership in its right form. Owning is often power and influence, and these two usually corrupt our mind easily. Only a few people can be poor when rich and rich when poor. Real freedom cannot be purchased. Either you figure it out or you don't. The means of substituting the true freedom are many—ownership is one of them.

# Relationship

Why do two people live together? This question came up today when my friend had some issues with his spouse.

The framework Martin Buber created in his famous book *I and Thou* in the 1920s is one way to treat the subject. Most of the time we are living in an I—It relationship with our world. The world around us has some purpose for us. We have created names (labels) and categories for various items, things, and actions around us. We have a perception of them and we think (i.e., we think we know) what they are. This works OK with ordinary functions and items but not so well with people. Still, most of the time we treat people like things. They serve a purpose for us.

Another relationship is possible and this is I—Thou way of being in the world. We do not try to categorize or label the other. We admit that we cannot know the other person entirely, not even talking about changing him or her. In addition, we are constantly changing, which means that nothing is static (i.e., our thought model will not be realistic). In an I—Thou relationship, we do not have any purpose, function, or "image" of the other person in our mind. We simply take the other as "fresh," how she or he appears and is. We both are what we are and discover each other every moment. This relationship can be achieved via a dialogue. In dialogue, both parties share and contribute by creating something between them that has no preconditioning or any expectations.

Quite a lot of marriages end up in divorce nowadays. We often hear couples explain the reason for the split as the other party changed or the couple just drifted apart over time. This could not happen in an I—Thou relationship where someone is not trying to get something from the other party. Nor is there any attempt to change or try to define the other person.

When we create an image of the other person in our mind, we also instantly create expectations and relationships. We create an object that serves a purpose for us. Everything is fine as long as the "image" in our mind matches with the reality. But it only takes a few moments before the other changes and shows some parts of his or her existence that do not fit to our "perfect" picture of the other we had created earlier on. When the illusion is broken, we get angry. We are disappointed or frustrated. Our image of the beautiful life together did not materialize. We had thought it through already (i.e., lived) in our mind and then we just should have had to live according to our predefined plan (i.e., imagination). When this does not happen, we blame the other. We did not expect this. We did not want this or we did not expect this to happen. The other has changed—how unfair! Is there anything or anyone we can rely on or trust anymore on these days!?!

Did we ever know the other? Did we actually have our own needs and illusions and dreams we wanted to fulfil? The other was just an object for those purposes. He or she came into the picture because I needed him or her to fulfil my dreams/needs. Maybe I was lonely, or needed to improve my self-esteem, or I was after wealth or security, wanted to fulfil others' expectations (e.g., relatives) of a socially acceptable life or I wanted to have a beautiful wedding or a family. Maybe I was after happiness because I was unhappy before. Being together was not enough in the first place. The question was not even about the other person. We disappointed ourselves. We failed our own expectations. The other person was just a vehicle for our own needs. Were there any possibilities for a lasting relationship after all—maybe everything went wrong from the first impression (thought)?

Relationships can work out only when we are not expecting anything from the other, ever, and when there is no need to be fulfilled or anything that is lacked. When just being is enough and no expectations are laid out, we can find love and happiness. A true dialogue.

# Sharing

It's amazing that there is enough of everything on our planet. The thing is that we create the scarcity situation with our own behavior. There is enough food to feed every hungry person and give each one a shelter, and even provide basic health care and education for everyone. These are the basic requirements for human life and they are doable every year. We just choose not to do these—collectively. We opt not to do anything and therefore we are also responsible of our actions.

Our lifestyle is based on individualism and egoistic self-fulfilment. We live by consuming and trying to satisfy our needs by material means. Our well-being is dependent on how much we can consume and drive after our whatever desires. Or that's at least the way we live. Are we happier and more satisfied? Are we ever satisfied and feeling content with our lives? In postindustrial society, we should already be more than happy with all the possessions around us.

Unfortunately, the reality is the opposite. We are more lonely and lost than ever. We have fulfilled our lives with cold values and individualistic lifestyles that isolate us from other people and make us lonely and unhappy people without much purpose and meaning in our lives. Isn't this strange because we now have more time off than ever? A few hundred years ago, almost all people were in one way or another tied up to agricultural work in order to support themselves. Now we do not have to exert so much effort to feed ourselves and get a roof over our heads. The problem seems to be more a mental one nowadays. We have time to think and worry—physical labor is not keeping us occupied anymore.

Almost everyone lives in isolation, even when we are surrounded by lots of people. Our lifestyle is very self-orientated. We have learned to live without taking into consideration other people's circumstances. How else could we explain that every day we see people who are more in need and lost in their lives than we are, but we pretend not to see them? We cross the street or at least turn our eyes away. Out of sight, out of mind. Secretly we hope that we could be so fortunate that nothing like that would ever happen to us. How coldhearted is our way of living? And for what? How happy and content are we really because we do not care about other people? Isn't this a clear indication of an opposite state of matters?

Sharing is an amazing thing. The joy and happiness inside of us is universal for all of us, that idea of being able to give something without expecting something in return. When was the last time you gave of yourself? It does not have to be a big thing. Just a smile or unexpected nice words to start. Everybody wants to feel accepted and respected as human beings. After all, we are all humans and what we have does not define who we are. How many of us are human in our actions as well?

Do we really need all the material things and wealth we have for ourselves? Isn't there anything we could share with those who are in greater need than us? Big changes happen with small actions. We are the society and the nations; there is no government or institutions without us, the people. Therefore, it is our responsibility to define who we are. Doing nothing and accepting things the way they are is as big a statement as anything else. By letting people starve to death and die because of poor health care demonstrate more than anything else who we really are. We are ignorant and selfish. How else can we explain these things? The technology is well developed and proven to prevent these things from happening if there is a will to accomplish it. It's done already in Western societies. No excuses—let's face who we really are.

The important question is, are we going to change? Personally each and every one of us has to look into the mirror and answer the question for ourselves—have I done enough today, really? If not, then there is still a chance that there is something human left in us, which we could try to make bigger in time. Maybe we would feel a bit more content and happier about our lives as well? It's give-and-take—sharing.

# Who Thinks?

How can we search for something we know nothing about?

How do we acknowledge or recognize the unknown?

We only know what we know. We only see what we know. We only hear what we know. But who knows, hears, and sees?

We categorize, conceptualize, and separate—this is our existence. Our existence is based on separation; we are apart from our perceptions. It's a binary world in which we're living. Either things are or they are not. I'm me and you are you. We are not the same. In other words, our existence is relative. We are only existing in relation to something (i.e., outside world; a rock, bird, house, person, etc.).

René Descartes said *Cogito Ergo Sum* (I think therefore I am). But who thinks? And what happens when we are not thinking. Thinking means that we categorize, conceptualize, put thoughts into words—something that is known. How can we think something new (i.e., something that is unknown to us)? Where do all the new ideas come from? (Who's the muse anyway?)

Krishnamurti might point you to the right direction. But thinking will only get you so far.

# Words

Our communication is mainly verbal—at least the visible one. We speak, read, and think in words all the time.

Let's get the basics sorted out first. We need conventions in order to communicate with each other. In traffic, we use traffic signs and lights to signal. We agree that some sign or mark means something and then everybody gets used to interpreting the meaning. This is actually the same with words as well. They are just a way of communicating and making things easier. By definition they are no more than alphabets in some recognizable order.

We take for granted that the symbols (words) we use are precise in nature. But the reality is the opposite. Everybody is living in their own perception of the world. The easiest example is to ask someone to describe the association of a word to be presented. For example, asking people to draw what we mean by a "chair" demonstrates that the drawings do not look even closely similar. And we haven't even begun to consider more complex and abstract concepts like globalization and freedom, to name a few.

A lot of misunderstandings and harm are caused by using words. People mean something and interpret it the other way—their own way. The most powerful words might be related to our religion, faith, and politics. Some of these symbols have gained a sacred status. The words have started to live their own lives. Their original purpose of describing and referring to the real issue has been forgotten or blurred somewhere in the process. Our history is full of "holy" wars and massacres for the "greater cause." Idealisms have become more important than human beings. By using words we can divert and disconnect the reality and get carried away by the pure power of concepts. In the name of these symbols we're ready to kill people and do amazing things. Seldom do people really ask about the basics and fundamental meanings of these symbols. Words are easy to use and even more easy to abuse. They are powerful and so precise in their outlook, but their actual meaning is mostly less simple and clear. And we live by getting confused by their looks.

# To Be

*To be,*
*how we are supposed to be,*
*believe the way we ought to be,*
*see what we want to see,*
*and pretend to be,*
*the one we have learned to be,*
*but that's not me.*

*So be,*
*and purely be,*
*without hesitation,*
*just be,*
*but realize to be,*
*truly,*
*simply,*
*be cause, to be.*

# Experience

# Parallel

*Different stages,*
*various levels,*
*intercepting each other.*
*Same moment,*
*different meanings,*
*present in all of them.*

*Separate paths,*
*isolated ways,*
*interlinked only for the few.*
*Reaching for the next,*
*struggling in the past,*
*worrying for the future.*

*Gaining experience,*
*the hard way,*
*is the slow and easy,*
*mostly used and favored.*
*Converting the current,*
*realizing the meaning,*
*living the truth,*
*is the instant reach for the will-*
*ing.*

*Gradual gains,*
*layered and stay,*

*remain for the next,*
*step for the greater,*
*further and brighter.*
*The future way,*
*of realization and gain,*
*better understood,*
*aligned,*
*without the strain.*

*Parallel,*
*here and now,*
*one within the other,*
*full of life,*
*isolated from each other.*
*All linked and acting,*
*planned to support,*
*and coach,*
*way to develop,*
*and progress,*
*up or down,*
*in or out,*
*heading forward,*
*never failing to drop out.*

# Dual Life

Our inner life is sacred and personal to each of us. Our external life we share with the world. It is not obvious that they can be in harmony and still enable the sought-for inner realization. But it is possible.

History has given us examples of sacred people who lived in isolated places and practiced their spiritual life. Often, we have this image of true practitioners, and nothing else is "serious" or real enough. Inner peace and mindlessness do not require any particular place or arrangement. We can practice it no matter where we are. It also stays with us when we have reached the right level. Actually, our environment and circumstances are no obstacles to our inner development.

We have to live in the world and take care of our duties and responsibilities. Actually, what provides a better opportunity to practice detachment and tranquility than the challenges of our everyday life? Our situations provide us with the training arena where we should be able to stay in a totally harmonious inner state—no matter what we are experiencing.

Living under time and space where causality is imposed does not mean that we cannot have a rich inner life as well. We can experience both worlds continuously. A place or situation will have no significance for us because our life is our state of mind. We create the meaning for the circumstances—not the other way around.

True teachings are nonverbal. They are not given by any symbols (i.e., writings, talk)—we have to experience them directly. Therefore, our life defines our existence, and by our behavior and actions we state who we are. What would be a better way to share the wisdom we have gained than to live among people and be a practical example? No words are necessary.

# High Stakes

Some of us choose a harder route. We want to achieve things faster this way than it would take on the usual long and less steep road. This means that we are put into a series of tests that are progressive in nature. They come in different forms and shapes. They drive us to our limits and press us hard. We are offered the easy way out, which means failure, but the real solutions are usually nowhere to be found and beyond our personal comprehension. Often, all the circumstances are against us. This is the harder way.

The rewards are high as well. Our life is very intense and rich in experiences. Situations may even seem strange to bystanders. Lucky coincidences and amazing turnarounds occur. We are not that surprised if we have the inner knowledge of the real issues. Anything is possible and at the end, things turn out the good way—if we only last to the end. The choice is ours and we can opt out. But there are a few of us who have made it all the way—they are the hope for the rest of us. They are very few in numbers, compared to the total population and even to the number of people reaching for higher grounds. But everybody is free to join—the choice is ours.

# Knowledge versus Wisdom

*"The wise are not learned, the learned are not wise."*—Lao Tze.

A wise person may not have much knowledge but a knowledgeable person is not wise. Wisdom is something that is intuitive—firsthand experience. Knowledge is based on words and descriptions. Knowledge can be acquired, shared, developed further, and transferred. Knowledge is not the same as wisdom. Wisdom requires insight and this "eureka!" cannot be taught by others. We can only help others on the road by explaining and sharing some knowledge about the wisdom.

We can convert wisdom into knowledge but this does not mean that the essence of the wisdom can be converted as well. It can only be described and illustrated with various symbols, anecdotes, and metaphors. Describing and telling about the road is not the road itself.

Often we want to gain more knowledge. We feel that we are lacking something and by acquiring some more knowledge we can get rid of our shortcomings. This is the pattern our thinking and behavior take. We need to attend a seminar, listen to a guru, or read a book. How many times do we stop to think and consider what we are really lacking and what the purpose of this knowledge "filling" is before we actually do anything? Because if we want to get better at something, then we should also make sure that we really gain the wisdom at the end of the knowledge acquisition. Otherwise, the whole exercise would be time wasted from the wisdom point of view.

How do we distinguish whether we have actually learned anything by acquiring more knowledge? Because wisdom requires insight this means that it is also reflected in our behavior and actions. Knowledge is converted to wisdom only if we are acting differently after getting the knowledge. This might sound more complicated than it really is. We can have a complete theoretical knowledge of how to drive a car but this does not mean that we can drive a car. Knowing the function of all driving instruments and traffic rules does not make us excellent drivers. We have to turn the knowledge into behavioral patterns and actions that are observable. Knowledge is easy to get but wisdom is a rare art.

Wisdom requires active participation and action. Learning can be done passively. It is harder to create a theory than describe one that is already formulated. We have a habit of learning more knowledge. The underlying assumption is that this knowledge is converted into wisdom as well. Unfortunately, the outcome is very often the opposite. The knowledge acquisition is our own illusion we so dutifully repeat time after time. We feel important and that we are doing something very meaningful and significant by learning something. For us, doing is often more important than the actual results. This is the unfortunate conclusion we must draw by observing the world around us. We love our illusion of knowledge and ignore the most important thing—the real deeds and outcomes.

# Levels

We are used to degrees. Our school years are based on num-
bered degrees. We live and breathe different steps and thresh-
olds. We have to qualify and learn the lessons before we are
approved to achieve the goal we are seeking. The same applies
to life as well; the scale is different and we can keep trying as
many times as needed. Everybody's learning curve and pace is
unique. Still, the goal is ultimately the same in each level—
some just jump from one level to another faster than others.

Our lifelong learning system is set up a bit differently than
the one we are used to in our own educational systems. Here
we have to try first and the reward or penalty is given later on.
The appraisal is not instantaneous, which makes learning
more difficult. This means that we are not quite following the
cause-reason causality anymore. Things seem to happen for
no particular reason or purpose. This causes confusion, which
is the real acid test. If we are to learn something, it has to be
verified in all the circumstances—otherwise it would be just
pure chance and not a conscious act of will. Learning should
not be based on lottery, should it?

Our level is preparation for the following ones. We get bits
and pieces of the forthcoming concepts but proportioned for
our own development and ability to handle them. These concepts are spread around the world in various shapes and forms
in a way that we run into them everywhere. We only have to
keep our eyes open and be ready to receive and notice them.
Some of them are more obvious and others are hidden more
carefully. Still, we recognize them and can put them into the
bigger picture like a piece in a big puzzle. Gradually, we get to
know more pieces and start to get a feeling of the overall concept. In tiny steps we improve our performance and learn some

important lessons—finally they turn into a part of our everyday life and existence. Then we are ready for other lessons.

Like when we were in school, we learn the alphabet and practice it so we can communicate. After a while of usage, we start to ignore the letters as such and focus purely on the message they carry. Often, we just forget that not everything we say or mean can be expressed in words. Also, some precise words do not necessarily mean that the very concept they express is as exact. Similarly, we express and learn some concepts and ideas derived from the next levels. They are not that accurate or entire—they can be only described with the alphabet and illustrations from our world. We need to translate and use allegories. Every translation and derivation also means that some information is lost in the process. The meaning is not as exact anymore and things can get confused and imprecise along the way. Therefore, the reflection of the original source is not the original but simply its representation or replica. Often, we take these copies as originals and get messed up in our mind. This creates a lot of confusion, agony, and misinterpretation. Still, we have to use these more-or-less precise concepts in order to learn our lessons. They are like toys and fairytales for children, harmless but they still serve a purpose—they are meant for education and learning. Like smaller children who are not yet allowed real items, similarly we are given a nice sandbox in which to practice things. Yet it seems that playing in the sandbox and getting involved with the concepts we are learning drives most of us off the topic for way too many moments.

Some of us get so carried away to play the game and form our sand houses and lives so that anything else is secondary. Big facades are torn down and sand grains thrown into other people's eyes are not that uncommon. A few of us are less concerned with making temporary monuments than gaining insight and knowledge for the more permanent foundations. These types of people are harder to find and they cannot be shaped like sand cakes. The tricky part is that we are given enough to make us masters at our level but the degree test is very hard and objective. The bar is high and it takes a relatively long time to pass the test. Eventually everybody will get promoted, but some are more ambitious in making progress than others. And a few have had enough of the sand games and want to move on. Fortunately, there is no limit to how many cakes we have to bake. Only the results count. And the weighting in the test is equal—for all of us. See you around!

# Our Teachers

Every one of us is here alone (but not necessarily lonely). We live among other people and yet all the great challenges of life we have to face alone. Our friends and people we keep close can support and give us the courage we need in our journey. Circumstances often take us on some rough rides but the greatest lessons are given to us by other people. Our life is about relationships with people. Some are strangers and just visitors in our lives and some are here to stay longer with us.

Our life is about learning new sides to and issues about ourselves. The things in our lives are purely about us. The people we meet, the situations we face—they are not coincidences or pure chance. They have a meaning for us and help us to get to know ourselves better. Still, it is up to us to do the work and learn the lessons. Often we are ignorant and seem to repeat the same patterns. We realize this when similar kinds of things happen to us. For example, we might get involved with the same type of people all the time—and they get us into trouble. Or we seem to struggle with our bosses in each and every new job we have. These things will happen to us until we acknowledge the pattern and learn from our behavior and actions. Then we are up to new challenges.

Other people play an important role in our lives. They are the mirrors for us. They interact with us and give us the test bed for getting to know our different sides and even hidden talents and emotions. People, through their behavior and actions, show us who we really are—and it should not be any big surprise that often we are the last people to see the reality. Just check with your closest friends—they may describe your other side if you only let them.

We get angry and frustrated with other people easily. They are the ones to blame. Why are we agitated? Why should their behavior concern us? Other people's problems or bad behavior are not our problem. So there is no reason to get emotional. Unless there is something in us that knows that they have revealed or awakened some hidden issues in us, such as ego, selfishness, laziness, greed for power, hypocrisy, and so on. Naturally we do not like to be reminded of those darker sides of us. We cannot stand it, and we blame others. As long as we have these issues with ourselves, we will need other people because we are not voluntarily working with ourselves.

Therefore, each human interaction and moment in our life is a new opportunity for us: to learn more about ourselves and become better human beings. Every person you meet is most of all teaching you about yourself. You only have to be humble and open-minded to realize the messages. Remember to thank the people around you. You don't have to say any-thing—just smile and love your neighbor. He or she is your greatest teacher.

# Reverse Confidence

Have you ever looked back on your life, thought about the incidents and situations you faced in your life? Often, the sudden and out-of-the-blue surprises that we are at first shocked by and terrified to overcome later turn out to be important turning points or stepping stones to something else. They did serve a purpose and were necessary in our pursuit for something else. In the very situation we did not realize the bigger picture, but later on, sometimes even years later, everything makes perfect sense. There was a red line after all. We just did not realize it earlier.

There are a few Hollywood movies that tell the story from the end to the beginning. The film *Memento* is one of these. For the spectator, this is a very annoying experience because the causal relationships we are so used to in our everyday life is working in reverse. The situation and things happening are not leading to something but are results and consequences of something that has already happened. Therefore, it is practically impossible to "know or expect" the next phases of the events.

Our life works this way as well. We can only track back the events leading to this point but the next phases are not known to us. This makes us insecure and uncertain about our future. Anything can happen—or that's the thinking.

We could use reverse-order logic on our life as well. We are very confident when looking back on our lives. The sense of security derives from knowing that finally everything turns out to be OK (because we are here to reflect back on our memories). Similarly, we also understand better the circumstances and may analyze the reasons and situations that we have already lived. But why are we so uncomfortable with our future? Why should it all change and things become unbearable for us suddenly in the future? Our activities in the past were necessary and led us to many surprises. Not all of them have been negative and many of them have actually given us something. We have learned from our mistakes and these experiences have given us new ideas and added new dimensions to our lives.

Look back on your life and focus on some important developments in your life. Can you claim that all the incidents and situations in your life have been totally chaotic and range from whatever unexpected irrational incident to another in no particular order, where putting it together makes absolutely no sense at all? Has all of it been a pure waste of time and resources? Pure chaos means that random events happen and each incident is not in any way interrelated or dependent on any other occurrence. Chaos consists of no logic but a hidden logic is no chaos. Reverse confidence may start to make sense. :-)

# Tranquility

Inner peace derives from an insight and internal knowledge and confidence. It is a known fact for the one who has realized it and, therefore, it is also a permanent state of being. One has to reach for and make a persistent effort to gain it, but when it has been achieved, no effort is necessary—you just are tranquil.

Inner peace or tranquility derives from the notion that one has realized that there is nothing to be afraid of. Everything is in order and our existence is pure love. In other words, the realized knows that everything is as it is meant to be and there is nothing that we are not expected to experience or face. All circumstances are meaningful (or meaningless). Nothing can happen to us that would not serve a purpose and be for our well-being. Life is love and so are we, as well.

Our confusion and distrust results when we are too afraid and scared to face life. We do not trust that it would support us. We have too much to lose and too much at stake. We cling to the reality we know and the perception we have. We freeze and hang tight to our mind and our concept of the world because we do not know anything better. Our illusion of being in control prevents us from being able to give away. And without totally letting go, we cannot gain the firsthand experience and knowledge, the internal realized trust. Until we have surrendered to life 100 percent, we will live in fear and mistrust. This is the paradox and the ultimate catch-22.

Nothing comes easily, but to realize the inner certainty and confidence we do not have to do anything. We already are everything—we only have to realize. We do not need time and effort per se—only personal insight is required. It cannot be faked and it cannot be done halfway only. Either you reach for your goal or you don't. The good part is that we get better and gain confidence while we're progressing. Regular practice helps us to intensify our realization and every step of the way we are getting closer. Inner peace is not about achieving or gaining anything. Therefore, it cannot be claimed but it is always waiting for us. We need only be prepared and ready for it—be humble in front of life.

# Written Meditation

We read many books during our life. The type of reading we do varies with the topic, our interest in it, and the situation. Sometime we just want to pass the time while waiting for something else. Holiday and travel reading are just some examples. On some occasions, we are very focused and concentrated on the text. The book is so good that we do not see or hear the world around us. Time flies when we "wake up" from the book's fascinating world. This state of concentration is meditating. Our mind is not wandering around but focusing on the text for long periods of time.

Our reading style is different when we study. We need to focus and concentrate in order to understand the context. It is more of a struggle than when we read a good fiction novel. Our mind tries to slip off from the concentration required for learning something new; reading in this way is work, like any other serious thinking processes.

When we study, we use the text and words as pure means to penetrate and realize the idea and concept illustrated by the words. We want to gain insight and learn the idea the author is trying to present and transfer to us via words. What we actually do is we use the text as our meditation tool. It is our guide and map to help us to reach the concept and thinking of the writer. Our concentration is in seeking to catch and reflect the thought object produced by the author. Some texts are easy for us to understand—we gain the insight and realize the meaning. Often, we have difficulties reproducing and reflecting the thinking, especially with subjects unfamiliar to us. We need to work hard to expand our mind in order to understand something new, unknown, to us.

We are able to learn and gain insight without firsthand experience. However, this does not mean that we should not actively strive forward for the insight. Pure mechanical read-ing does not provide us with anything. We simply mimic and repeat the mantra of the text without catching the concept and the idea transferred by the text. In other words, we might gain some knowledge but definitely not any wisdom. But wis-dom can be achieved and realized from written materials. This is an excellent way of gaining insight. It only requires that we are open and willing to learn and are persistent: noth-ing comes without personal responsibility and effort. The most important component is our personal desire and humble attitude toward learning more about ourselves. With practice, we get better and our meditation technique improves as well.

# Detachment

*The view,*
*so vivid and exciting,*
*full of life,*
*happiness and joy,*
*sometimes sorrow, often pain,*
*from limited knowledge and*
*ignorance,*
*glances still;*

*Stepping back,*
*enlarging the scope,*
*gaining new foothold,*
*spectating,*
*from a distance,*
*different angle;*

*Firmly pacing,*
*knowing,*
*from here I must walk,*
*these curtains must fall,*
*something must go;*

*Giving away,*
*the known,*
*to make space,*
*for the unknown,*
*letting go,*
*to fall,*
*the facade,*
*so dear and attached,*
*which does not hold,*
*it must go;*

*The one behind,*
*was an angle of mine,*
*based on defects,*
*that was all,*
*nothing really at all,*
*but it was all,*
*I knew.*

# Qualities

# Happiness

*Is a moment of joy,*
*a smile or a kind word from a*
*stranger;*
*Unexpected and spontaneous,*
*innocent.*
*Beauty of the vision,*
*perfectness of the glance,*
*the vulnerability of the*
*inevitability,*
*it all happens right here and*
*now.*
*How to reach for the inner*
*state,*
*the feeling of comfort and lov-*
*ing kind;*
*To experience the life,*
*as it comes;*
*by humble mind and open*
*arms,*
*you are always welcome,*
*I am here to stay.*

*My lesson is to learn,*
*the sorrows and the pains;*
*but also the glimpses of glam-*
*our,*
*and the highest of the scale.*

*One day happiness will*
*become,*
*the same as sorrow;*

*My time will come,*
*when this is true;*
*Then I am ready,*
*and will see;*
*Two sides of the same coin,*
*minted into one;*
*No more happiness,*
*no more blue;*
*They are here,*
*but not for me;*
*I have learned,*
*and see them through.*

*All was for one,*
*greatness of life;*
*that beyond the scope,*
*let us reach;*
*and finally teach,*
*to give away,*
*for all we know,*
*nothing more to stay.*

*The stage is different,*
*and the tools as well.*
*Good-bye we say,*
*and leave without a trace.*

*Happiness*
*is here to stay.*

# Forgiveness

Our life is full of incidents and situations where we are strongly emotionally attached. These occurrences can have a significant impact on our behavior. We can feel deeply involved with something but still have little understanding of the real drivers and motivation. It is not uncommon that we even know deep inside that we should act differently than the way we are acting in practice. Still, there is something in us that is forcing us to a certain kind of behavior.

Attachment is a sign of fixation and pattern that is deeply rooted to us. We have a strong standing point in something— great expectations or emotional affections. These sensations may not be very logical and sensible to us, but they have a power to overdrive our cognitive understanding and will. Some intensive occurrences can make us to feel very confused and fixed to the current state of being.

Often, we are very hard on ourselves. We expect more from ourself than we do from others. It is easier to forgive and give away to other people than forgive ourself. This makes our life hard and difficult. Our internal contradictions and expectations drive us to hardship and struggle. We blame ourself and get frustrated when things are not in our control. Strong emotional feelings are something we have a hard time keeping in control. They can even blind us, causing us to act against our normal sense and better understanding. Especially in these cases, it is important to let go and forgive ourself. Emotional feelings are strong signals of our inner state and, therefore, should not be missed. We have to take them into account and overcome them. Our feelings cannot be forced under our cognitive will. We can only try to understand and forgive. They are to guide us and let us learn more about ourselves. Great lessons sometimes require hard methods.

Therefore, forgiveness is very important and necessary. What we do for others we should also do for ourself—forgive and start with yourself.

# Humbleness

Our life is full of low and high moments. In the great moments, we have a feeling of being in control and having some special qualities. In the blue moments, we feel insecure and imperfect. Usually we reflect our qualities and self-image based on the activities and outcomes around us. We draw quick conclusions and create causal relationships with the outcomes and our own contribution to the events. These evaluations are subjective and are dependent on our perception of the issues. Unfortunately, we can only observe things from our perspective and without better understanding of the actual relationships and reasons for the matter. This continuous appraisal, which can be more or less subconscious, cumulates and supports our own personal development for better or worse.

In the extreme, false, continuous interpretations of situations often lead to dramatic disappointments and incidents that restore us to the reality. We have to face the fact that we might not have been as great or clever as we have thought. Something unrespectable or unfavorable happens for us that contradicts our understanding and perception of the reality. This comes as a shock to us but not really to the people around us. We are usually the last person to realize this. Our loved ones and people dear to us may have tried to warn us in various ways, but we have not taken these indications as something of great relevance. In other words, our self-image has let us down.

We cannot escape the fact that we are bound to experience life with subjective judgment. We are imperfect and our perception of the world is not objective. Our understanding and perception of the world changes over time. We are more or less ignorant despite our best intentions. In fact, each human being is trying his or her best but because we are different, the degree and level of ignorance varies greatly among human beings. These differences create the disruption and conflicts among us. If our perception and knowledge would be totally aligned, there would not be disputes and issues between us. In other words, we all would possess exactly the same qualities and similar understanding of all the issues.

Humbleness means that we are aware we are not perfect. We admit that "we are only human"—we do make mistakes. Many of our faults are materialized even when we are not aware of them. To realize this, we must also comprehend that other people make mistakes as well. They do not intend to do so but like us, they simply are not aware of their own short-comings. They are in the process of learning about them-selves. Every one of us is in a different position and situation in this learning process and we need other people and the sur-rounding world to get us to become aware of and realize our mistakes.

Almost without exception, we are offended when someone tries to teach us about our shortcomings. We do not like to take advice from other people. We should know our own business better than everyone else, especially when the response is not very nice or polite. We get emotional or angry and this can lead to actions and consequences we may regret later on. From another point of view, our behavior results in something that offends or is not correct from the other per-son's point of view. We may have not intended this but just simply cannot realize it ourselves.

Humbleness lets us live our lives and learn about our qual-ities without judging other people in their shortcomings. Being humble about our own behavior and actions acknowl-edges that we are like children who are still learning about life. We are not very knowledgeable, and there are others who can teach us more. Because we are still so inexperienced and ignorant, we are in no position to give any advice or offer opinions of other people's behavior. We have so much to do with ourselves that it would be ridiculous to advise others when we are not capable of coping with our own lives and being a perfect role model for ourself. A master is responsible for his or her teachings and, therefore, should advise only in matters in which he or she completely excels. How many of us can claim to master life?

# Patience

We are used to living in the world of instant action and response. Each generation claims that the current speed and flow of information is almost too much to bear. The stress we feel, which is imposed by our society, the closest ones, and our working life, is almost too much to handle. So what is all this fuss about? Who's in a hurry and why?

We feel anxious when things seem to move too fast for us. We are not focused and cannot exactly draw the full picture. This is something very personal and subjective. Air traffic controllers have a different meaning of stress than kindergarten teachers and extreme sports base jumpers have. What is common to everyone is that the external activity level and the inner state of patience and calmness are totally different issues. When we are feeling comfortable, we can achieve a lot without any distress.

With experience and practice, our comfort zone extends. We learn to separate our physical existence from our inner state of being. With time, we start to feel less concerned about the circumstances and even new situations facing us. No matter how fast the pace or strange the situation, it should not affect our inner being. Those are just issues to deal with—no big deal.

We start to perceive life with patience. Everything has its time and place. For some activities we get involved, and for others we do not; sometimes our presence is required for an activity, and for some activities our presence is not necessary. Our time will come if we need the experience or the capability. Our life gives us what we deserve, but we are often just too impatient to wait for it. We get anxious and start to act on our own. And then we are confused. Things get out of our control and beyond our reach. At this point, we need even more patience.

Greater patience also means that we are in better control of our lives. Consider a while before acting. Take a deep breath before saying anything. Listen first and think your thoughts through. There is plenty of time to analyze the situation. Observe and notice your surroundings. It's amazing how much you can improve things by delaying your reactions by just a small moment. Often your outcomes may turn out totally the opposite of what you expected—for the good. Have patience—and consider for a while before rushing for other more "important" tasks.

# Harmony

*A state of indifference,*
*existence without significance.*
*Way to be the world,*
*let others see the perf.*

*How to describe something,*
*where two ends meet and never leave.*
*Enough,*
*no more, no less.*
*Just the opposite,*
*of everything that whines or cries.*

*No need, no lack,*
*kind order without slack.*
*That's the way,*
*but how to stay?*
*We achieve,*
*and never be.*
*Which results that,*
*harmony,*
*is something we,*
*top for this,*
*and gain for that.*
*The swing pendent,*
*never stops,*
*for a perfect harmony.*

# Index

978-0-595-37522-6
0-595-37522-7

Printed in the United Kingdom
by Lightning Source UK Ltd.
110784UKS00001B/58-138

9 780595 375226